MULTIVITAMINS FOR THE MIND

Nirmala Raman

Qurate
quratebooks.com

MULTIVITAMINS FOR THE MIND

Nirmala Raman

Published in 2024

© Published by

Qurate Books Pvt. Ltd.
Goa 403523, India
www.qurateboooks.com
Tel: 1800-210-6527, Email: info@quratebooks.com

ISBN: 978-93-58986-85-3

Prologue

When my son asked me his everyday question,... "Mom, have you taken your multivitamin today?", and, knowing my answer fully well, brought along with him, a multivitamin capsule and water, a thought provoking question sprang into my mind. How do I convince the younger and the next generation that if the mind is strong and healthy, it will take care of the body also? I'm not against these health pills and tonics. It's only that I believe more in a stronger form of 'medication', which, along with physical health, takes care of the all important mind and gives you a greater immunity, in the form of inner strength, peace and happiness.

And, as an apt answer to that question, this book was born. The various essays in this book will act as a trigger to enlighten the mind, thus making one healthy and peaceful, both in body and mind.

So, now I bravely retort to my son "Have **you** taken your mental dose of multivitamin today?"

Contents

Preface

Stop! **Pause** a bit!! **Ponder** a while to analyse yourself and your life. Do you know **who** you truly are; **why** certain things happen to you or **what** you can do to enrich your life? If it's a 'No', then this book is for you. If it's a 'yes', then also this is for you! Now **Proceed**!

The essays in this book are not to tell you what to do and what not to do. Nor is it a book of thrillers or sci-fiction. It is merely a collection of various eye openers, to bring an awareness of some of the valuable aspects in yourself, so that you can **Pause** a bit, **Ponder** a while,

Inquire, Introspect and finally **Proceed** towards your journey, to the Glorious path of serene tranquility. The various topics dealt with are not an affair of a few months, but the dedicated efforts and results of more than a decade of reflections, surveys, references and notes taken from the talks and books of various spiritual and vedantic masters and gurus.

There are some things in life, which you do, just because of a strong urge or the pull of an unseen force. This book belongs to that category. I was fortunate to have a collection of the Great thoughts from the lectures and books of various Spiritual Masters, and decided to organise my years of spiritual tid-bits collection into a consolidated whole, and share it with whoever was interested. It would be constructive, selfless and a fulfilling work. And it certainly was! When I started going through and studying deeper on topics like these, my thoughts elevated and I could get a deeper insight of my True Self. It was like taking doses of multivitamins for the mind!

It's my strong belief that you readers, partaking of this tonic will reap rich rewards.

Nirmala Raman.

1

Our 'Constituents'

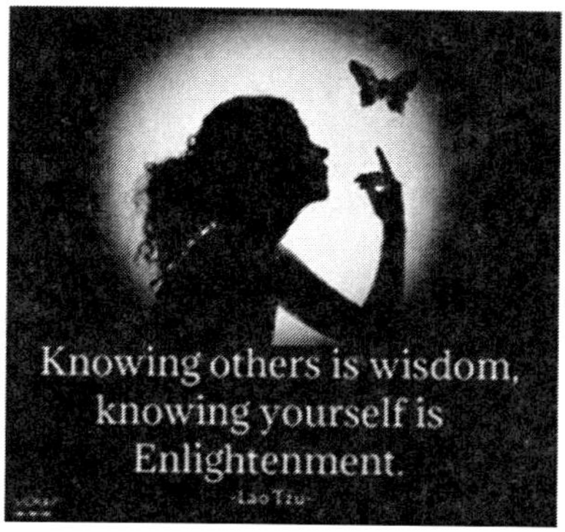

Most of us are aware of the constituents of so many things around us, like the chemical constituents of water or air, or the materials needed to build the house. A chef very well knows what ingredients go into the making of his different dishes; a great singer knows the nuances of his song. But how many of us have a true knowledge of our ownselves or even cared to ruminate about the ingredients that are within us? Most of us are very well aware of our physical selves- the human body, (including the brain), its various systems, organs, glands, their secretions and functions etc. But, how many of us have ever given a thought to "Are we just our physical bodies, made up of flesh and blood, with the various organs and systems doing their immaculate work"? "Or is there something beyond?" We say that we see with our eyes, hear with our ears, work with our hands and so on. But can the eyes really see, or the hands really work? Certainly not! If we remove an eye or a hand, can they see or do any action at all? They become useless. Hence we can conclude that there is something beyond all this which enables the eyes to see or the hands to work. This is the Enlivening Force within us, and this is our Real Self. Thus, we are much more than our physical self. We are something far beyond who we thought we were - a mere Mr. X, with a degree, job, family and so on. We are a part of that Enlivening force, a part of Awareness- which is The Divine Principle, that pervades the entire cosmos, and enables everything to function. No wonder that our great seers and sages of yore, having analysed thoroughly 'the real we' unequivocally declared that we are not just the body with a soul, but in reality, a miniscule of the Universal soul trapped in a body! What a fantastic statement! With their profound knowledge, they have declared that every individual is composed of Matter and Spirit. The material aspect comprises the physical body, (consisting of the 5 elements - pancha bhoothas-, i.e earth,fire,water,air and space), the mind and the intellect, whereas the Spiritual aspect comprises the Soul/Atman/God Principle/Divinity/ Consciousness /Awareness.

THE MATERIAL ASPECT: consists of (a) The physical body (the visible part) has 2 sets of organs - 5 organs of perception (eyes, ears, nose, tongue and skin) and 5 organs of action (hands, feet,organs of speech, reproduction and excretion). (b)The Mind and Intellect (the invisible part of our material aspect) which is more subtle, cannot be seen or touched, but only experienced. Various emotions and feelings pertain only to the mind. That is why we are told 'it's all in the mind' and advised to train the mind to nurture only good thoughts, and root out the harmful ones! (In spiritual parlance, mind is also called the heart). The intellect is closely associated with the mind, and is the discriminating faculty in us, responsible for making us think, judge, reason and analyse between right and wrong. It is these two -the mind and intellect, (influenced by the vasanas)- that defines our personality -makes us who we are. The faculty of the intellect should be the guiding factor to the mind, as the mind is like a monkey and is the seat of various feelings and emotions and is easily carried away. It has to be carefully watched over and policed at all times by the intellect and hence the intellect should be so nurtured that it is available to us at all times to efficiently guide the mind in the right direction. (Swami Chinmayanandaji compares the mind to a child and the intellect to a mature adult, who has to constantly police and steer 'the child' towards the right path).

THE SPIRITUAL ASPECT: This is the REAL SELF within us, the Atman -that Divine, True, Unchangeable, Consciousness or Awareness factor, within each of us that enables us to live. It is that God Principle, that Enlivening Force which causes all our organs and faculties to function. (It is also called SACRED SELF or HIGHER SELF by Dr Wayne Dyer). We cannot see It but we know that It is there. Our great spiritual masters compare this Divine Principle and Its function to electricity and the various electrical gadgets. Just as electricity is the main factor responsible for the functioning of all the gadgets, but at the same time is NOT RESPONSIBLE for the efficiency or inefficiency, use or misuse of the gadgets themselves, similarly, the Atman in us-, is a mere Witness, or a Sakshi, and is not responsible for our good or bad actions.

Our ancient Sages and Seers, through a deep scientific study and analysis, formulated the spiritual-physical personality of a human being. Accordingly, the Divine Spark of life, the Atman, has 5 layers of matter enveloping it, called Kosas or Sheaths. (Panchakosas).

1. The outermost Food sheath or Annamaya kosa, containing the 5 organs of perception and 5 organs of action. (gross)
2. The Vital-air sheath or Pranamaya kosa, consisting of the 5 pranas- the activities which support the body take place as a result of the air that we breathe. They correspond to the

modern physiological systems, responsible for the faculties of perception, excretion, digestion, circulation and thinking.

3. The mental sheath or Manomaya kosa, consists of a steady flow of thoughts. It is also the seat of emotions and feelings.

4. The Intellectual sheath or Vigjnanamaya kosa, is the storehouse of all memory and knowledge.

5. The Bliss sheath or Anandamaya kosa. (most subtle), consisting of vasanas or imprints. It is made up of ignorance in which we exist during our deep sleep state, and is blissful as we do not experience any agitation as is felt in the other 2 states of consciousness- wakeful and dream states.

However, these 5 sheaths have no separate existence as such, and dealt with only for our understanding. And all these 5 layers are mere matter and hence inert. It follows then that there should be something more than this, that gives consciousness to these inert things. This is called as the Atman/life Principle/ Consciousness/ Awareness/ Divinity or simply God.

The word Atman is a Sanskrit terminology, that refers to the Self or self existent essence of individuals, as distinguished from the ego, mind and embodied existence. It is the Universal Force, that enlivening factor which is all pervading and giving life to everything.

We can broadly think of Atma as (a) The Pure Consciousness or Awareness (called Purusha) found everywhere at all times, and is known as **Paramatma**, and (b) when a speck of this Universal Paramatma comes in contact with the matter (called Prakriti), it enlivens the matter and gives rise to an individual. This embodied Atma in an individual is called **Jivatma.** This Jivatma within us, transmigrates along with our subtle body (mind and intellect, along with our vasanas or unfulfilled desires), after death, to another new body. (For a Self realised person, the Jivatma joins with the Paramatma and attains moksha or liberation from the cycle of births and deaths). The role of the Atma is just like that of a Witness. It is not responsible in any way for the good or bad actions of an individual. The purpose of our lives on this earth is just to seek That Atma, That Divinity within us, by removing the layers of ignorance surrounding our True Immortal Self.

Once we have a basic knowledge of ourselves, it becomes clear that this body, mind and intellect to which we have been clinging on till now, is just one aspect of us, the inert and temporary aspect, and that the more important Permanent aspect within each of us, is our Spiritual aspect, our Real Self. This realisation is the first step and, the sooner we detach ourselves from the notion that we are just the Body, Mind and Intellect, and start to associate, attach and propel ourselves to the Higher Reality in us, the faster will be our progress. Sages, Seers, Saints and many enlightened men have all vehemently asserted this great Truth- Swami Vivekananda had declared : "There is a power of God in every man". Dr. Radhakrishnan had reiterated, 'Every human being is a spark of the Divine". Let us also try to get enlightened by constantly reminding ourselves of our Divine Nature and tapping and drawing on the Great Potential Force within us- The Spiritual or Divine Force, pervading the entire Universe and beyond.

To empower us in this journey of enlightenment, we shall take the first dose of the multivitamin and then climb the first step of the Inward journey, by embarking on the All Powerful Prayer.

Hari Om Tat Sat.

2

Prayer

"MORE THINGS ARE WROUGHT BY PRAYER THAN THIS WORLD DREAMS OF"

Prayer is just an act of empowering **your own self.** It is a simple, but sure, means by which you align yourself with the mighty Power of the Universe and be in tune with It. It is a sure fire way of communicating with The

Divine within and without you and establishing an intimate link between both. It enables you to experience The Real you.

From this perspective, human beings can be categorised into three types. The first type **are the simpletons,** who have undoubting faith, belief and devotion in a Power higher than themselves, which they call God, and, very devotedly pray to Him/Her, making use of the very Powerful prayers and hymns, written by our great Masters. Their worship may involve pujas, rituals, pilgrimages and so on. Even their relationship with the Divine is unique. Some assume the Power to be a Divine Mother, who showers abundant love on her children, or a Protective Father, or a Loving Spouse, or a Bosom friend with whom he can share all his joys and sorrows. This is similar to the same person being called a father, mother, sister, brother, child, friend etc, by different people, according to his relationship with that person.

Though God is only One Formless Entity present everywhere and encompassing the entire Universe and beyond, the great seers of ancient times, knowing man's love for outward pursuits, had given various concrete names, forms, and attributes (Saguna aspect) to the One same abstract entity, (Nirguna aspect) in order to proceed from the known to the unknown. Thus he starts befriending the Divine,in a known form as portrayed in books or mythology- Lord Rama, Lord

Krishna, Devi Durga and so on. Sometimes they have a special God as their favourite (Ishta Devata). (like Meera for Lord Krishna, or Ramakrishna Paramhansa for Goddess Kali). This is a good strategy, as there is more focus and intensity. If the practice of praying starts from childhood, the faith and belief gets firmly rooted and continues to remain steadfast, even during adulthood, when other priorities have to be met. After his active physical life of transactions recedes, he once again gets into a routine of devotion, worship, pujas or pilgrimages. Life and its challenges are easily met since he has the backup of faith and trust in a Super Power, who will never let him down.

This simple and easy path of attaining the Divine through pure love and devotion is known as **BHAKTI YOGA**.

The second group of people are the rationals,to whom mere prayers to a God they haven't even seen, do not appeal. Being more of a physically active worker,they would rather DO something concrete, That's fine too. Their path would be to tirelessly and without selfish motives, work dedicatedly towards the common good. 'Service to Man is Service to God' or 'Work is Worship' would be their motto. Our scriptures go one step further. It gives the assurance that even if one does their daily job or studies in a focussed, sincere and dedicated manner, without craving only for the rewards, but as an offering to The Divine, it is considered as a high form of prayer. Lord Krishna in the Bhagavad Gita says "Whatever you do, by thought, word or deed, do it as an offering to the Divine'. This alone will enable one to reach the Absolute. This allowance will certainly be a boon to the student and career building groups, as they have neither the time nor the mentality to pray to an unseen God. Of course the condition should be that the study or work done should be dedicated and sincere,and in a spirit of selfless service. This path to reach the Divine is termed as **Karma Yoga**.

The third group of people belong to the Intellectual type. Their passion is to inquire, study and contemplate on the Highest Truth. The great Saint Sri. Ramana Maharshi is perhaps the best example of having reached Self Realisation through this path- the path of **Jnana Yoga**.

One must remember that all these three paths are not mutually exclusive. There should be a beautiful blend of all the three disciplines. There are other spiritual disciplines also that hasten the process of our progress. Pranayama, Yoga, Mantra Japa and Meditation are some priceless tools in this inward journey.

Prayers are resorted to when one wants to get in touch with that Higher Power- either for its own sake, or for guidance, for solace, for strength, for gratitude, for removal of problems or asking for boons and so on. However, it is also mandatory that prayers should always be accompanied by Self effort. 'God helps those who help themselves'. It is not that problems will disappear; problems will still be there, but you will get the inner strength to face them boldly. Another important factor is that prayer will not give you all that you want- 'you will get only what you deserve and not what you desire'. To pray is our duty. What we receive in answer to our prayers has to be accepted as the Divine will- since we really do not know what is good for us.

The long term benefit of Sincere and Steadfast Prayer is the awareness that the person is also a spark of the Divine and that he is actually the Soul harboring the body and not vice versa. Thus, he tries to go on relentlessly pursuing his 'inward journey', to realise his True Self. Very soon he discovers that all the prayers were actually not to some mysterious God in Heaven, but to that Absolute Divinity, that Awareness, that Consciousness, that Super Power, pervading the entire universe. In this manner, he empowers and aligns himself more and more to that Super Power within him. There are other short term benefits too: Stress is greatly reduced, since you are not handling your problems alone, And when stress, the No,1 killer is reduced, automatically your BP, heart rate and breathing, normalises. It also gives one great confidence, and humility, teaching you the lessons of Acceptance and Surrender. There is great peace of mind and one becomes more calm, and cheerful, positivity increases while negativity reduces.

Above all you have started on your Inward Journey of becoming more empowered spiritually. .

Let's continue this journey with another great spiritual discipline- Prana and Pranayama.

Hari Om Tat Sat.

3

PRANA- The Life Force

(To be read in conjunction with the article 'Pranayama".)

Have you ever heard that all of us have, not One, but Two breathing systems? Surprised? Well, this is one more of the great mysterious Truths that our ancient sages and Masters had discovered way back. (The modern scientific world is still exploring this profound knowledge).

The first breathing system, the respiratory system, that we are all familiar with, is just the gross aspect.

There is a second and far more important breathing system in us,which is the subtle aspect. And that is the **Pranic breathing**. This is so subtle that it cannot be seen or heard even by the most powerful microscope! **It can only be experienced!** This powerful **Prana** has the mysterious capacity of enlivening all the 100 trillions of cells in the human body, directly, **without** going in a circuitous way like that of our gross respiratory system.

No wonder then, that this Prana is called the Universal Life Force, The Vital Energy, Breath of Life, etc. It is known in other cultures as well- Chi in China, Pneuma by the Greeks, Ki in Japan, Mana in Australia, and Aka in Egypt. It is the foundation of all life, animating all our thoughts and actions, and the cause behind the energy of the whole universe! It is Nature's gift to us and available in plenty, all around us.

The function of Prana is immeasurable. **At the personal level,** it is the source of all movement in the body. It regulates all of our conscious and unconscious bodily functions like our breath,our heart beats, digestion, blood flow, release of the various hormones and juices in our body, elimination, and cellular growth and healing. Prana also animates and affects the quality of our thoughts, emotions, and consciousness. Prana distributes its energy throughout the body based on the quality and capacity of the **NADIS (**energy channels through which the Prana flows), and the chakras (energy centers). Our overall health and well being is tied directly to the quantity and circulation of prana in our body. Even when we feel "tired" and "low", it is only because of our insufficient or imbalanced Prana. **At the Cosmic level,**It is the cause behind all the energy of all the forces (physical and mental) around us- Even heat, light, electricity are all manifestations of Prana. Prana is the link between the physical and astral body. When this slender thread like link is cut off, the Prana withdraws into the astral body and, the astral body separates from the physical body- i.e the body dies. "It is not only the basic life force but also the original creative power,". said David Frawley.

The Prana reaches our body only through breath. Breathing is the main form of pranic activity in the body. Thus by controlling the act of breathing, (Pranayama,) one can control the subtle Prana inside. The breath, controlled by the mind and will, is a powerful vitalising force that can be used for self development, healing oneself, etc. And when you control the Prana, You can control the mind, since the vibrations of the Prana alone produce the thoughts in the mind. **"The mind gets clear and pleasant through the controlled inhalation or exhalation of one's life's Pranas "- Patanjali's Yoga Sutra.**

Let us now examine this Powerful Life Energy or Force. Prana is distributed through every cell in the human body (there are millions of cells in the human body), through a complex system of 72,000 energy channels or NADIS. These are very subtle and cannot be seen or heard by even the most powerful microscope or stethoscope. Among the many nadis, three are most important- **1. The Pingala Nadi**, which governs the physical functions and is associated with the solar and positive energy, **2. The Ida Nadi,** which governs the mental function and is associated with the moon and negative energy and **3. The Sushumna Nadi,** which conducts the Spiritual energy that connects us to the Higher Consciousness. Diseases and mental disturbances occur when there is an imbalance, interruption or blockage to the free flow of the pranic energy in the body. **Pranayama** is the fastest and most efficient way to recharge the Pranic system and thus relax the body and mind. It purifies our Pranamaya Kosha or Sheath (refer the article "Pranayama"), and ensures the free flow of Prana inside the nadis or channels.This flow of energy of the Prana, is called **Prana Vayu.** Though actually a single unit, it is divided into 5 categories, depending on the location, movement and function. Accordingly, we have **Prana, Apana, Samana, Udana** and **Vyana**. All these forms can be strengthened by various Yoga Asanas or postures.

1. **Prana** -seated in the heart, provides energy to all the glands between the (anahata)-heart and (visuddha)-throat chakras. It provides the basic energy, governs all kinds of reception into the

body, (like respiration,eating, drinking), sensory impressions and mental experiences. At the psychological level, Prana governs our positive feelings and thoughts of the mind and senses. When unbalanced, it causes unhealthy desires and cravings. All backward bending yoga asanas are useful.

2. **Apana-** seated at the base of the spine, provides energy for all the glands between (muladhara)-root and (svadishthana) -sacral chakras. Function is elimination (stool, urine, semen, carbon di oxide, and governs expulsion of fetus, during reproduction. At a deeper level, it governs the elimination of negative sensory, emotional, mental experiences and is thus the basis of our immune system. Apana governs our ability to remove negative thoughts and emotions. When unbalanced, makes us suppressed and weak. All pelvic asanas activates Apana.

3. **Samana**- seated in the navel, provides energy to the adrenal gland and aids digestion of food, absorption of oxygen in the lungs, and mental experiences. Samana gives us contentment and a balanced mind, while a lack of it brings us greed, attachment and possessiveness. Asanas of twisting the body activates samana and is beneficial to reduce body fat and control diabetes.

4. **Udana**- is seated in the throat and is responsible for swallowing, balancing the thyroid gland, and governing the growth of the body. It is our main tool for positive energy. It separates the spirit from the body at the time of death. Rotation practices are useful for Udana energy.

5. **Vyana** is the reserve energy and responsible for blood circulation. It moves food, water and oxygen throughout the body and gives strength and momentum to our thoughts and emotions .

Apart from this, there are also 5 sub Pranas- **Naga** (eructation and hiccup), **Kurma** (opening of the eyes), **Devadatta** (Yawning), **Krikara** (hunger and thirst), **Dhananjaya** (decomposition of the body after death). The Golden Key to good physical and mental health is to keep all our Pranas working in full harmony.

How can we increase Prana, and also conserve and channelise it?

Increasing Prana: Nature is the Best booster for Prana. Anything Natural- food, air, sunlight, greenery- all these increase our pranic energy. Along with this, doing Pranayama-esp. Nadi Shodana (Alternate Nostril Breathing), a few Yoga Asanas, and having an erect posture, are all greatly helpful. Proper Nutrition- vegetarian diet full of life- force, like fresh green vegetables and fruits, sprouts, whole cereals is also important. Having a positive mental attitude, like, consistent love, empathy, forgiveness, acceptance and release, laughter, music, and above all, a pure mind rooted in ethical values will all tremendously increase the Prana Power within you. Mantras like 'Om' help create vibrations that can help positive energy and finally, Meditation- the Greatest of them all, is the ultimate promoter of Pranic energy. (If you are a sincere Meditator, you can even start experiencing the free flow of Pranic energy within you and can mentally direct it into specific parts of the body, if needed.) **"Meditation is the ultimate gateway to life force "Prana". Meditation opens all the closed inner gates in the spine and brain that bring power to your body, mind and soul. When you meditate your body becomes filled with electricity, or life energy that is present in the ether (space). Meditation is the turning on of the inner switch that fills the body with the divine current."- Sri Paramahansa Yogananda.**

Your Prana energy will keep on flowing within you, as long as you keep purifying it. All the above methods will be of no use, unless you embrace the nature of Pure Love and have no negative thoughts about anyone, or, your own life in general. The more Pure your thoughts, the freer will be the flow of the Pranic energy within you.

You can **conserve Prana** by not wasting it on useless and unnecessary things like gossip, worry , stress, and having negative feelings- anger, jealousy, hatred, revenge, etc- towards others

You can **channelise Prana** by your good actions and thoughts. Selfish thoughts and actions only deplete the prana energy in you, but selfless thoughts- kindness, empathy, thoughtfulness of others, service to others, gratitude, forgiveness etc,, will certainly increase the powerful Spiritual Prana. This should be our goal.

The **miraculous effects** of the free flow of Prana within you, can be seen when : 1. you find that things that affect other people do not bother you much. 2. There is great support from Nature/Universe towards your endeavours. 3. Complex situations get resolved without much effort. 4. You become more peaceful and calm, and even if there are some agitations or hardships, they do not last long. 5. Many undesirable tendencies and happenings drop off effortlessly. 6. Circumstances somehow become conducive to your advantage. 7. Minor ailments and illnesses get cured by themselves, due to an increased immunity system. 8. Your resilience towards problems increases greatly, due to the great increase of an inner strength from within. 9. Ability to focus and concentrate increases greatly. (There may be more!)

There is Infinite Power within you. We are much much more than our mere Physical bodies. We are That Spark of Divinity, covered by the body- not vice versa. However, most of us cannot see this Truth. Nor can it be explained. It can be understood and experienced only by people who have felt the free flow of Prana energy, effortlessly, within themselves. Let us resolve to Increase our Pranic Energy, and unleash our true potential, without further delay. A great way to do this is by **Pranayama.**

Sources : divineyogabangkok.atavist.com, Swami Sivanada Saraswati, Yoga Basics, Sri. Paramahansa Yogananda.

Hari Om Tat Sat

4

PRANAYAMA... Small Investment - Bounteous Returns

Let us now take the next Multivitamin Pranayama and explore the benefits.

Pranayama is a practice of directing the energy through the breath. It aims to control the breath, making it deeper, slower and longer, thus extending and enhancing life.

Pranayama is so simple, and yet so very powerful, but unfortunately, very few practice it. This is mainly because many of us are ignorant of the wonderful benefits of this simple act of breathing, which we anyway perform without awareness, every moment of our lives! All we have to do now is just spare 10 to 20 minutes of the day, at any convenient time and perform the same act of breathing, but with a little awareness. This is what Pranayama is all about! .Literally the word 'Prana' means Life force and 'Ayama' means regulating. The Sanskrit word Prana, is translated as physical breath or vital force and at a deeper level refers to the energy of Consciousness itself- the original creative power.

Sri Daya Mata, Disciple and Successor of Paramahamsa Yogananda says "Pranayama is the bridge that one must pass over to get from physical consciousness to this divine awareness within". David Frawley in his article "Understanding Prana" says "To bring about positive transformations in body and mind, we must understand the energy or force, PRANA, through which they work.

The human being consists of 5 Koshas or sheaths-

1. **Annamaya Kosha-** (made of food). This is the physical body, composed of the 5 elements- earth, water, air, fire, ether)

2. **Pranamaya Kosha** (made of breath). This is the vital body, composed of 5 aspects of Prana, called Vayus.

3. **Manomaya Kosha** (made of impressions). This is the outer or lower level of the mind, filled with the 5 kinds of sensory impressions.

4. **Vijnanamaya Kosha** (made of ideas). This is Intelligence itself, directed mental activity.

5. **Anandamaya Kosha** (made of experiences). This is the deeper mind, containing the memory, the subliminal and superconscious mind.

Out of these, the second sheath, **The Pranamaya Kosha** is the sphere of our life energies, and is composed of the 5 pranas or vayus (forces of air)- **Prana, Apana, Udana, Samana,** and **Vyana**, according to their movement and function. In brief, they work in unison, like an efficient machine- Prana brings in the fuel, Samana converts this fuel to energy, Vyana circulates the energy to the various parts, Apana disposes off the waste products produced by this conversion process, and Udana manages the energy thus created! The key to good health is to keep our pranas working in harmony. The body and mind, which are linked by the Prana, are purified by regulating the Prana, and the main method is the purification of the channels or nadis, through which the prana flows. Prana is distributed to every cell in the body through a complex system of 72,000 energy channels called nadis. Among the many energy channels, there are 3 main ones called Pingala nadi, Ida nadi and Sushumna nadi. The first one conducts the energy which governs the physical functions (and is associated with the solar and positive energy); the second governs the mental function (and this is associated with the moon and negative energy); the last conducts the spiritual energy which connects us to the higher consciousness. As they all are closely connected, the unhindered flow of Prana through all the three is necessary for spiritual awakening.

According to Sadguru: If one takes care of his Prana, there is no such thing as physical ailment and much less, psychological imbalances or mental disturbances

Pranayama is also a system of techniques used to harness and regulate the universal energy, Prana. It is the fastest and most efficient way to recharge the pranic system and by doing so relaxes the body and mind.

We have all studied in schools that when we breathe in, or inhale, the oxygen from the air enters our lungs, purifies the blood, and, (through our nostrils, and goes to the back of the throat and into your windpipe or trachea. This divides into 2 branches called bronchial tubes, enters the lungs and further divide into over 300 million tiny branches called bronchioles each of which ends in an air sac called alveolus (plural alveoli). The alveoli are surrounded by a mesh of tiny blood vessels called capillaries. Here the air is purified through a process of exchange of gases- oxygen is taken in from the alveoli to the blood and carbon dioxide is given out by the blood to the alveoli- and the purified oxygen rich blood is carried back to the various parts of the human body. Similarly,) And when we exhale, the impure air, rich in carbon dioxide, (which has been taken away from the blood), is expelled.

But, this is just one part of the story. When we breathe in, there is another and more important activity that goes on. In addition to the oxygen, we also take in a lot of Prana (the vital force that makes up the entire cosmos). While the oxygen gets diffused in the lungs and then gets into the blood stream, and from there to the various cells, the Prana takes a shortcut- it travels directly and reaches every cell in the body, through a system of thousands of subtle 'nadis' (tiny channels - similar to the blood vessels in our circulatory system), energising it and giving it the life force. Thus Nadis are the pathways and Prana is the vital energy flowing through them. (Thus we can say that we have TWO breathing systems in our body!) Nadis are not a part of our physical body and cannot be seen even under a microscope. They are a part of our subtle energy bodies, and can only be experienced. It is said that we can live for many weeks without food, days without water, minutes without air but not even a fraction of a second without prana!

What exactly are the benefits of Pranayam?

When we learn and regularly practise Pranayama, we begin to use the entire lungs. We can take in and expel seven times more air, oxygen and prana than our normal quota of 500 cubic centimeters that we do in our normal breathing! Oxygen is a great necessity but Prana is THE BEST booster for our good health. Thus, in Pranayama, we are literally taking in gallons of vitality and immunity, and enriching our blood with life force. No virus can enter and expect to flourish! Yes, it is a great healer. Pranayama not only eliminates toxins from the body and blood, it also purifies the nervous system, making the mind alert and aids in digestion and sleep. It helps in curing asthma and other respiratory disorders, and heats or cools the body as needed. It charges the body with extra energy, builds stamina and resistance. It can provide you all the nourishment you need and reduce your dependence on food or medication. This is the physical benefit.

Your mental energy and state can also be boosted. Breath reflects the condition of the mind. When a person is agitated, tense or angry, the breath is shorter, faster. When fear is present, the breath is heavy: when depressed or sad, the breath is a deep sigh. However, with the change in the breathing pattern the mind can also be changed. The breath and mind are closely connected. (Thats why people tell you to hold your breath and count upto 10 or to take deep breaths whenever you are upset or angry.) Pranayama can easily and effectively change an agitated and stressed out person to a more calm and composed one. It also provides one with more mental strength, and consequently he can easily face and tide over the challenges of life. It is one of the easiest and best tools to remove the negativity and increase positivity in the mind.

At the Spiritual level, this practice will certainly hasten the realisation of his Divine Nature, since the body, mind and spirit are an integral part of each other and stay closely inter connected.

Through prolonged practice of Pranayama and Meditation, one can become aware of the subtle flow of the prana energy through the various nadis, going to the different parts of your body. This pranic force or energy can then be directed mentally to any part of the body or even mind. In this manner one can, to an extent reduce body aches and pains, tension, and at an advanced level, even minor illnesses, or mental agitatiations!

There are different types of Pranayama exercises.

Though all Pranayama or breathing exercises are useful, the alternate nostril breathing (Nadi Shodan) is the most important method for keeping our pranas or energies in balance. This is because, according to the yogic system, the right side nostril and the nadis are solar or fiery in nature (dealing with activities like digestion, work and concentration) while the left is lunar or water predominant, (dealing with rest, sleep and relaxation). It is said that at any given point of time air goes in only through one nostril more predominantly than the other, and this changes every few minutes and in order to balance the flow equally on both sides of the nostril, Nadi Shodan is needed. Three other important pranayama exercises are:

- **Bhastrika**- bellows breath.
- **Kapalbhathi** - skull shining breathing.
- **Bhramari**- bee breath.

The mandatory need of the hour for every human being is Pranayama. Any excuse, however valid it may seem, is unacceptable. We have to learn to prioritise, and give Pranayama the first priority. It alone brings harmony between the body, mind and spirit, thus making the body healthy, the mind clear and peaceful, and the spirit greatly empowered. It is a bountiful ocean of pure nectar, from which we can partake easily and freely. On the edifice of this basic, strong foundation we can achieve great heights. What more convincing does one need?

Next, we shall explore yet another discipline- Mantra Japa.

Hari Om Tat Sat.

5

MANTRA JAPA

Though I have been practising Japa for many years, it is only very recently that I understood the deep meaning and significance of this great Spiritual Science and Spiritual discipline.

Japa is actually the repetition of a Mantra. 'It trains the mind to fix itself to a single line of thinking', said Swami Chinmayananda. A mantra can be just a single syllable, like 'Om' or a single or many names of any Divinity of one's choice- Vishnu, Rama, Krishna, Shiva,

Devi, Jesus, Mohammed etc. It could also be a group of words- Puranic mantras like " Om Namo Narayana", "Om Namah Shivaya", "Sri Ram Jay Ram" "Hare Ram Hare Krishna " etc. There are also Vedantic Mantras like 'Tat Tvam Asi' (That Thou Art), Aham Brahma Asmi, (I am Brahman), Shivoham Shivoham, (I am Shiva) and Puranic Mantras like 'Om Namo Narayana', Om Namah Shivaya. 'Hare Rama Hare Krishna' Whatever it is, it is just a symbol of that One Great Divinity, that Pure Consciousness permeating everywhere. Thus a mantra is Divinity itself, enveloped in a structure of sound. (Of course you should do the Japa with a deep feeling of the Divine and with the knowledge or meaning of the mantra.) Japa should be performed with all intensity, sincerity and regularity.

Many saints and sages like Sri Ramakrishna, Swami Vivekanand, Holy Mother Sri Saradha Devi, Swami Brahmananda and Mahatma Gandhi, have practised and advocated this discipline.

As mentioned earlier, a mantra repeated many times constitutes Japa. Japa can be either a loud repetition (Vaihkari Japa), a mere muttering(Upamshu japa) or a silent repetition(Manasika japa) of a mantra, done with the aid of japa malas or rosary made of rudraksha,tulasi sandalwood, lotus seeds or even pearls or crystal beads... usually 108 in number. Right ring finger supports the mala, middle finger and thumb help to move the beads. After repeating the mantra 108 times, you reach the

Guru bead, called Sumeru, and if you want to continue, you turn the mala, to repeat and not cross the Sumeru bead.Though the Brahma Muhurta time, 4.30 to 6.00 am, and a quiet spot in the house are the ideal time and place, mantra meditation can be done at any convenient time and place. Sitting posture, whether in padmasana position on the floor, or sitting erect on a chair are both fine. Another wonderful form of Japa, is the writing down of the Mantra, also called Likhita Japa. Starting at a very early age, and continuing even today, whenever things go beyond my control, I fervently resort to my favourite likhita japa- "SriRamaJayam" and it has worked miracles! There is great advantage in this, as there is control over your posture,your mind, sight and tongue,and a very special joy of writing- forming words with your pen on paper! There is certainly more Concentration and less Distraction of the mind in this form of japa, as one has to observe silence and intense focus while writing this.

The effectiveness of Japa to a large extent depends upon the spirit of surrender. Swami Chinmayanada says, 'Surrendering or Prostrating is not merely the physical act of bowing. It is a conscious act of discovering the greater in us and seeking our identity with it. To tune ourselves with the better or nobler and gathering unto ourselves the very qualities and greatness of the higher, is true prostration'. One surrenders his matter-conditioned false ego unto that unconditioned eternal Self which is also within us.

'Repetition of a mantra has a mysterious power of bringing about the manifestation of the Divinity, just as the splitting of an atom manifests the latent forces within it', says Swami Shivananda. Now, since words are associated with forms, Japa will inevitably bring its form to the mind. (When you repeat any mantra, the Divine form or picture will appear in your mind as 'thought'. This one pointed thought of His Divine form constitutes DHYANA. This is a form of meditation. Though you start practising with both the japa and the Dhyana, at a Higher stage, the japa falls off and the meditation alone remains.

The repetitive name of Divinity, when dwelt upon continuously, creates a God-Consciousness in the purified mind. Though the utterance should be without mistakes, allowance is given for unknowing mistakes and shortcomings. As Sri. Krishna says in the Bhaghavad Geeta, "No Spiritual practice ever goes in vain"! Japa and Dhyana are the means to the realisation of God Himself or, more accurately, towards Self Realisation.

What are the benefits of Mantra Japa?

To put it in simple terms- **for the purification of the body, mind and heart.**

Japa brings forth a calming influence, which has been proved scientifically as well. A hospital in Barcelona experimented this on patients, before surgery and found that there was an increased alpha activity of the brain, heart rate and BP returned to normal, and the anaesthesia needed was only 50%! Medical scientists have found out that it increases the formation of Nitric oxide in the nasal cavity, (cells function much better) and secretion of Colony stimulating factor (better immunity to fight diseases), Melatonin (for cheer, enthusiasm and happiness feeling), Endorphins (that act as natural analgesics), and Vagus nerve stimulation (to take care of the steady functioning of all organs).

Japa is a definite means of Self Realisation. Sri Ramakrishna says "When you chant the mantra, (eg. name of a Diety) with single minded love and devotion,you become absorbed in Him and realise Him." According to Patanjali, regular repetition of 'OM' (the Supreme Sound- the Sound symbol of God) leads to the awakening of the Self.

Japa/Mantra has the Sacred Power to **liberate, and protect us from pyschophysical, moral and spiritual dangers.**

Japa leads to deeper meditation. A japa conditioned mind is a great aid for a meditator to reach unimaginable heights in a very short time.

It also subdues the lower nature in us and enhances the Higher Nature. With the reaching of the Higher Consciousness, all nature is seen as Divine Consciousness.

When Mantra japa is thus constantly practised, (no fixed time, duration, place or any other restrictions are needed for this), it becomes an automatic, subconscious habit by default, and will be remembered even at the time of death, (a great privilege given to only a few!) ascertaining a Blessed Place even after death.

In case one is not able to actively practise Mantra Japa, one can take recourse to the **listening of any great mantra** as often as possible, like the Gayatri Mantra or the Sri Vishnu Sahasranaama Mantra (1008 names/ attributes of Lord Vishnu) or Sri Lalitha Sahasranaama.

Mantra Yoga is an exact science. In Hindu religion, a Mantra has 6 parts- **a Rishi**,(Self realised soul or Seer) to whom it was revealed for the first time and who gave it to the whole world, (Sage Viswamitra is the Rishi for the Gayatri Mantra, Sage Veda Vyas for the Vishnu Sahasranaamam etc); **A Metre or Chhandas**, to govern the inflexion of the voice; **a particular Devata,** as its informing power; **a Bija or Seed,** that gives special power to the Mantra-it is in fact the essence of the mantra; **A Shakti,** which is the energy of the form of the Mantra; and **a Kilaka**- the pillar or pin which plugs the mantra-chaitanya that is hidden in the mantra. Constant and prolonged repetition of mantra removes the plug and the Chaitanya that is hidden in the Mantra is revealed.

Is there anything more that needs to be said to convince one of this easy, simple but highly effective spiritual discipline?

Let us now take the extremely beneficial multivitamin and proceed on our sacred inward journey towards the greatest spiritual Discipline- Meditation.

Hari Om Tat Sat.

6

The Power of Meditation – Part 1

Having been a sincere and ardent meditator for more than 25 years and enjoying abundantly the Peace, Bliss, Serenity and other great benefits derived from it, I do feel it would be unfair and even selfish, if I do not divulge its miraculous powers to others. Why should we Meditate? In a single sentence- to Empower us Physically, Mentally and Spiritually.

So far, all our lives have only been an outward journey. Either we are in pursuit of worldly needs and pleasures, "Getting and Spending, we lay waste our Powers" said William Wordsworth, or, we are greatly engrossed in acquiring worldly knowledge. Science and technology have made vast leaps and bounds. We have even conquered many aspects of outer space. They are certainly laudable. But sadly, ironically, how many of us have even an inkling of the inner space within us? How many have tried to even peek into the space within us? Our sacred space? The space which is eternally our very own- our True nature? Worldly transactions, with people and situations; pains and sufferings due to the trials and tribulations of the past, anxieties and stress to make and fulfill plans and aspirations for the future - these alone have been the hallmark of our lives. Our minds are always agitated by past or future events. Thoughts of worldly objects or people, incessantly keep bombarding our minds. And, as long as we are attached to the world of objects, we are bound to be smothered by the thoughts of them. We get 'STUCK' to the pain or pleasure it brings. Both are harmful - even pleasure, since anything outside us, being transitory in nature, cannot give us lasting happiness. Welcoming pleasure, but not getting attached to it, accepting pain but not getting bogged down by it- this alone is the right attitude. "Pain is unavoidable, but Suffering is Optional" said Dr. Krishan Chopra. True, this is not easy. It requires great determination, mental maturity, and a great disciplining of the mind. Freeing the mind from the continuous flow of thoughts, is perhaps the most difficult task. To achieve this, and maintain a state of equilibrium, we have to embark on our Inward Journey. Meditation is just that! All our great scriptures and Masters of yore,with their vast years of study and insight gained by light of their direct knowledge of a Higher State of Consciousness, have unequivocally declared that Our true Essential Nature is Divinity, and realising this fact is the basic goal of our birth in this world. Unfortunately, we are not even aware of It because of the material layers of the body, mind and intellect,surrounding It. We continue to ignorantly attach ourselves to these superficial layers and consequently suffer the pangs of existence. Unless we slowly learn to detach ourselves from this transient, false self and simultaneously, attach ourselves to the Higher Reality/Consciousness/Awareness/Our true Self, within us (which incidentally is there in everyone of us- sinner or saint) we can never expect to experience Bliss and Peace. It may be difficult to give up that worldy identification that we have been used to all our life. But it has to be done. A simple method would be to just catch on to a higher aspect or more noble aspect. The lower automatically falls off! It has happened throughout our lives, but without our conscious knowledge. As a child, we were so attached to our toys. Later on, video games became the focus. When we caught on to that, the lesser thing- the interest in toys-dropped, and so it continued. Similarly, if one holds on to a higher and more noble ideal, the lower tendencies drop off on their own. Try to hold on to the Higher power within you- and slowly you will realise that everything else in you- is of much lesser value. The best aid for this is Meditation; for it is this alone that can take you to that innermost depth and give you a glimpse of the realisation of who you truly are!

Harnessing the Mind is a Herculean task! Our mind, which is nothing but a steady flow of thoughts, can toss us into strong currents of turbulence at a moment's notice! It is the main reason for all our problems. All our negative thoughts lead to frightful emotions of fear, hatred, jealousy, greed, anger,stress, tension etc which, in turn lead us to perform harmful and wrong actions. Consequently our whole personality becomes wrecked! There is no easy way we can control our thoughts. They are like a terrible monster, waiting to devour us and we helplessly succumb to this powerful force. Not only do these unhealthy thoughts rob us of our peace and serenity, but endanger even our all important physical health. There is a direct link between our thoughts and our health. Sir William Osler, a founder of modern medicine emphatically stated that our mind has a lot to do with recovery or otherwise in illnesses. Every doctor can vouchsafe for the connection between stress, anger, hatred etc and B.P, diabetes, ulcers and other psychosomatic disorders. Even our Immune system which guards us against diseases weakens with negative states of mind caused by negative thoughts. The one and only weapon for the 'Taming of this Shrew', is

Meditation. It is only in Meditation that the thousands and thousands of thoughts (majority of them are usually useless or harmful ones, of course) get slowly reduced and by constant practice, the mind settles down, even if it is for a few moments initially, to quietitude and an awareness OF THE MOMENT. No regret of the past or anxiety of the future can find a place in that Haven . Even the thought pattern or quality, changes to one of bliss, and a sense of deep love permeates the entire being.

When is the best time to meditate?

Our scriptures have said that the ideal time would be from 3.30 to 6 am. But if this is not suitable to the 'night birds', the next best would be at any convenient time, when you feel rested and alert. Probably after you get up in the morning, and before you have a heavy breakfast or get into the rut of the stresses and routines of another busy day. The benefits of this is that it acts as a protective layer and keeps you in a better mood to face the challenges of the day. Above all, it assures a consistency of practice, which is more important than timing.

How often and how long should one meditate?

There is no specific rule for this. Though it is recommended that you start with 15 minutes once or twice a day, a hard core meditator will meditate for more than 40 minutes. It all depends on one's convenience and the time available. In fact, today, there is a strong recommendation to have mini meditations as often as possible, just for 2 or 3 minutes, anywhere, anytime and any bodily posture. The logic behind this is that the calm and serene effect it produces, is carried on throughout the course of the day.

There are many types of meditation and relaxation techniques that have different meditation components. There are also different organisations and masters who can initiate and guide you. Their techniques may be different,- some stress on a blue light, some stress on breath, others on observing thoughts... and so on. Different paths, but their goal and benefits are all one and the same - achieving inner peace and calm.

It is always best to go to a trained teacher and get initiated on a one to one basis, with a personal mantra. Till then one can start by just sitting quietly with in a calm place, with eyes closed, erect spine, comfortable and relaxed position,either squatting on the floor or on a straight backed chair, or stool, not on a full stomach or a sleepy state and mentally uttering the mantra "Om". Thoughts will surely come, but don't worry or analyse them. JUST WATCH THEM WITHOUT JUDGEMENT AS THEY COME AND GO. DO NOT PARTICIPATE IN THEM. Remember, you are neither the mind, nor the thoughts. They may be yours- what you possess, but certainly not You. Use the Mantra to help you remain without thoughts, even if it is for a few seconds. By regular practice, you will improve. Personally, I have undergone the Transcendental Meditation (TM) course, including the advanced course of Maharishi Mahesh Yogi, and find it very convenient, as there is no rigidity in religion, beliefs, or timings, seating, (floor or chair) though it is very important to keep the spine erect. The process itself is simple, and the experience, profoundly refreshing and Sublime.

Some meditation techniques are:

1. **Guided Meditation**- Where a teacher guides you in visualising mental images of relaxing thoughts, using your senses- like smell, sight etc.
2. **Mindfulness meditation-** where there is an increased awareness of the present moment. You focus on what you experience during your meditation- like your breath.
3. **Mantra meditation-** where you silently repeat a calming word or thought to prevent distracting thoughts,
4. **Transcendental Meditation**- a simple natural technique, where a personal mantra or syllable given by an authorised teacher or guru is silently repeated . This form of meditation allows your body and mind to settle into a state of profound rest and relaxation. You just observe

your thoughts and allow them to pass, without passing any judgment.

5. **Tai chi**- This is a form of gentle Chinese martial arts training. In tai chi (TIE-CHEE), you perform a self-paced series of postures or movements in a slow, graceful manner while practicing deep breathing.

6. **Yoga-** You perform a series of postures and controlled breathing exercises to promote a more flexible body and a calm mind.

7. **Pranayama**- Simple breathing exercises, that promote deep relaxation and simultaneously increase the oxygen capacity of the lungs.

We all have an Infinite Potential within us. Meditation is a spontaneous way of allowing the mind to go inwards and harness that potential. The more you meditate, the Higher you rise. The calm serenity which can be observed in meditation, may be for a few moments initially. But, it will gradually increase with constant practice, and will then spill out gradually into our everyday life. This serenity will empower us to face any adversity with equanimity and with courage. An added bonus is that the calm and tranquil effect of a single meditator, will spread to the others in the family! Life will certainly become more peaceful and Joyous. And above all, guided by the Divine Super Power, Nature and circumstances will give a strong support and become very conducive to us!

Meditation takes practice. Thoughts Will come, but try not to be bothered by them or judge them. Just let them pass. Remember, there's no right way or wrong way to meditate. What matters is regularity. Meditation helps you to slowly realise your true Self in the long run, and reduce your stress and feel better overall, within a short span. Even 15 minutes of deep meditation is far more beneficial than a good nights' sleep. The body is enlivened, strengthened and rejuvenated. There is more clarity and focus. Emotional strength increases and you become more resilient towards life's challenges. The mind is more calm and relaxed, enabling the whole backlog of stresses to dissolve naturally; when the mind is relaxed and stress reduces, physical health improves; and above all, spiritually, you are on the path of the great Realisation of your True Essential Divine Nature! There is hence, absolutely **NO EXCUSE NOT TO MEDITATE.**

A word of caution- Don't judge your meditation skills. Or compare the results or experiences of your meditation with that of the others. Each one progresses at different speeds.

Meditation is not the prerogative of any one religion. It is actually the culmination of all religious rituals. In Prayer, You are talking to God. In Meditation, "God is talking to You", says Dr. Krishan Chopra (father of Dr. Deepak Chopra) in his book, "Your Life is in Your Hands". Let us resolve to start Meditating, and allow

God to talk to us. There is a lot of research going on throughout the world on this ancient Indian technique. Let us find out what they have to say, in our next lap of the journey- Meditation- Part 2.

Hari Om Tat Sat.

7

The Power of Meditation – Part 2

Meditation originated in India, long long ago. Though the mention of it in the written form is from 1500 BC in the Vedas, the Vedas themselves were memorized and passed on orally for centuries before that. Buddhism, Taoism, Jainism, Christianity, Zen Buddhism, Sufism, Jews and many Greek Philosophers- all of them have their own meditation techniques. In the modern world, Mediation has become a great Spiritual mantra, thanks to the famous Indian spiritual teachers like Swami Vivekananda, Paramahansa Yogananda, Maharishi Mahesh Yogi and Swami Rama. The practice of meditation became more westernised and infused with scientific research. The studies revealed that along with the eastern benefit of spiritual enlightenment, it was also highly beneficial for the body, mind and overall wellness, as it not only increases various useful hormones needed for a healthy body and mind, but also decreases the harmful ones. In some cases it can be more advantageous than medication, as it is a Natural cure, without any harmful after effects. No wonder it has become the new Mantra today.

A few global research findings and the views of some experts in the field of medical psychology are: 'If stress has you anxious, tense and worried, consider trying meditation. Spending even a few minutes in meditation can help restore your calm and inner peace'- global Mayo clinic.

Meditation has been practised for thousands of years. Meditation originally was meant to help deepen understanding of the sacred and mystical forces of life. These days, meditation is commonly used for relaxation and stress reduction.

Meditation is considered a type of mind-body complementary medicine. Meditation can produce a deep state of relaxation and a tranquil mind. It can give you a sense of calm, peace and balance that can benefit both your emotional well-being and your overall health. You can also use it to relax and cope with stress by refocusing your attention on something calming. Meditation can help you learn to stay centered and maintain inner peace.And these benefits don't end when your meditation session ends. Meditation can help carry you more calmly through your day. And meditation may help you manage symptoms of certain medical conditions.'

Emily Boynton, in her article "How Meditation Affects Your Brain and Boosts Well-Being" says: Mindfulness meditation is the practice of nonjudgmental, intentional awareness of the present.It can strengthen areas of your brain responsible for memory, learning, attention and self-awareness. The practice can also help calm down your sympathetic nervous system.

Over time, mindfulness meditation can increase cognition, memory and attention. It can also decrease emotional reactivity, stress, anxiety and depression."

In the article written by by Zameena Mejia, reviewed by experts, and published by Forbes, she lists 10 science backed benefits of meditation- Stress reduction, anxiety and depression management, lowering BP, Strengthening Immune System, improving memory, regulating mood, increasing self awareness, addiction management and improving sleep.

Dr. Jeremy Sutton in The website Positive Psychology.com, states: Meditation trains your attention, helping you to be more present, find peace, and savor positive emotions. Meditation connects the mind and the body, bringing mental and physical peace. The effects of meditation are far reaching, positively impacting our physical health and our mental wellness, including cognitive functioning and emotional control.

Matiz et al., 2020; Galante et al., 2021: Studies show reduction in : Anxiety, Depression, Stress levels, Job burnout

Kennedy Institute found that those who meditated regularly, had a 65% increase in their dopamine levels.

Rutgers University researchers discovered that melatonin levels for meditation practitioners were boosted by an average of 98%, with many participants having increases of more than an incredible 300%!

Clark University researchers: The results of the researches show that meditation can significantly affect hormones and neurotransmitters such as cortisol, dehydroepiandrostrone- DHEA, serotonin, melatonin and epinephrine.

According to the global institute, EOC, Exploration of Consciousness Research Institute: The analysis of findings from electroencephalograms and functional magnetic resonance imaging (fMRI), used to record brain activity, suggests that the "practice of meditation triggers neurotransmitters that modulate psychological disorders such as anxiety" (Krishnakumar et al., 2015, p.1)

Other research also confirms the impact of meditation and mindfulness on the brain.Regular practice calms the amygdala – part of the brain associated with emotional regulation and impulsive reactions to stressful events (Mindfulness, n.d.).While meditation is found in texts dating back thousands of years, modern research findings continue to shed new light on its potential to help us maintain good mental and physical health throughout our lives. It has also identified 141 uses of meditation in the Physical, Mental, Emotional and Spiritual fields. According to them, this ancient practice upgrades 7 critical brain and body chemicals. **.1.Serotonin**- Increases this "Happy Neurotransmitter". Most of our approximately 86 billion brain cells are influenced by serotonin. Serotonin is the key to help relay signals from one part of the brain to another. This crucial chemical has a profound impact on our mood and greatly contributes to our overall state of well being. University of Montreal scientists (Perreau-Linck et al) feel that meditation bathes neurons with an array of feel good chemicals, effectively melting away the stress that leads to low serotonin levels and depression. **2. Cortisol**- Reduces this Stress Hormone, which not only blocks the creation of good hormones, but is also responsible for the disasters like anxiety, depression, BP and so on. A study by a Rutgers University doctor discovered that meditators had a nearly 50% reduction in their cortisol levels. **3. DHEA** - boosts this longevity molecule. DHEA is one of the most important hormones in the body. As we get older our DHEA levels decrease year after year, opening us up to disease and accelerated aging. Luckily, meditation provides a **dramatic boost** in **DHEA** hormone levels. Dr. Vincent Giampapa, M.D., former President of the American Board of Anti-Aging Medicine and current prominent longevity researcher, discovered that meditation practitioners have an incredible **43.77% more DHEA** over everybody else! **4: GABA**- boosts this "Calm Chemical" — Best known for making you **feel calm**, GABA (gamma aminobutyric acid) is one of the major inhibitory neurotransmitters in your central nervous system. If you are struggling with a bad habit then it's virtually guaranteed that your **GABA** is depleted. Not having enough of this super-important chemical can create an array of problems, including anxiety, nervousness, racing thoughts, and sleeplessness. Luckily, there is an effective solution. In 2010, Psychiatrists at the Boston University School of Medicine found a **27% increase in GABA** levels after only 60 minutes of meditation. **5. Endorphins**-boosts this "Euphoric Neurotransmitter" that is responsible for the **all-encompassing** sense of **happiness** we sometimes feel. Endorphins are a category of neurotransmitters that the body uses as an internal pain killer. More Endorphin Benefits: Increases Happiness, Well being, Self esteem, Confidence, Motivation, Will power, Relaxation and reduces Stress, Bad habits and Chronic pain. **6: GH -The Growth Hormone-** increases this_"Fountain of Youth". The body's diminishing supply of growth hormone causes the frailty that comes with aging—weaker bones and muscles, increased body fat, poor heart contractions, bad moods, lack of motivation, and fatigue. Meditation effectively turns the clock back. **7: Melatonin-** Increases the "Sleep Molecule". A chemical "Superhero", melatonin is known to strengthen the immune system, slow down aging, and has been linked to helping prevent over 100 different diseases. Luckily there is a very effective, all natural solution. Incorporating meditation into your life can be your much needed biological re-balancing tool. More benefits of Melatonin: Reduces Depression, Anxiety, Headaches and Migraines, Diseases and Increases Immunity, Healing, Cell renewal. It is also a great antioxidant.

Meditation Is The Best Antioxidant. Backed by 117,000 peer reviewed scientific studies, meditation has been shown to boost 'glutathione' (GSH), the Huffington Post anointed "mother of all antioxidants." The benefits of GSH span the seven great seas. So, what are the experts saying? **Gustavo Bounous MD, retired McGill University professor told Medicinenet.com** that "It's the [body's] most important antioxidant because it's within the cell [which is prime position to neutralize free radicals"]

Jeremy Appleton ND, a naturopathic physician and respected author quotes, "glutathione is extremely important for maintaining intracellular health. Glutathione not only hinders oxidative stress, but also plays a helper role for many critical enzymes, fights cancer by slowing apoptosis (programmed cell death), boosts t-cells, shields environmental toxin damage, guards against drug resistance, while super charging immunity.

So, whether you are an old timer, who faithfully believes in the wisdom and practices of our ancient Rishis, or whether you belong to the modern generation which needs scientific proofs for everything, both will now realise the Power of Meditation- the vehicle that takes you inside. Let us now travel inwards and explore further.

Hari Om Tat Sat.

8

The way Upwards is Inwards

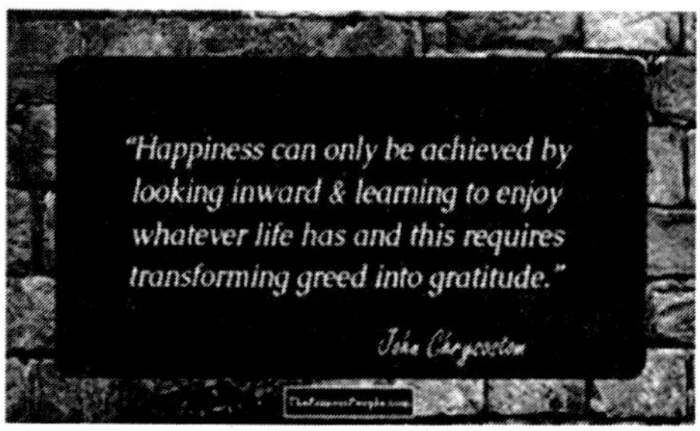

All our lives, we have been looking outwards for happiness and fulfilment. Quite natural, as our sense organs have been structured that way. The eyes see whatever is outside, the ears hear the sounds outside and so on. The mind too is constantly looking for and perhaps even finding the 'so called' happiness and pleasure outside. This is not wrong, as the outside world has been created for our enjoyment. The problem arises when we do not know where to draw the line and get lost in the mad pursuit of worldly pleasures.

Unfortunately, the happiness when a selfish material desire gets fulfilled lasts only for a short time. Again the mind wanders in search of something more. This 'drama' of the mind goes on and on. That permanent happiness goes on eluding you. Finally, there comes a point in a sensible person's life when he seriously starts wondering...'what is the use of all this? What is real happiness? Is this vicious circle of 'wanting, searching and finding, wanting more and searching again', the whole purpose of life? This unrest in his mind, is the FIRST STEP towards his upward goal in life. As long as man is hankering after outward pleasures- money, fame, power, comforts, etc, he will continue to be in the rut of pleasures, pain, disappointment, frustration, yearning, greed, loss of peace and a host of other maladies. It is only when he realises their shallowness, and becomes dis-satisfied with the external material pleasures that he starts searching for true and lasting happiness, and thus takes his first step towards Enlightenment. Thankfully, we have a host of great thinkers, sages and philosophers, from times immemorial, who, through deep contemplation and divine revelation, discovered and gave us a whole lot of precious literature and guidance in this sacred journey. They have indeed given us the GOLDEN KEY to unlock this sad state of affairs.

Almost unanimously they have all revealed that TRUE HAPPINESS LIES WITHIN. It is just a State of the Mind. Any amount of wealth, fame, possessions or other material things may give you a little temporary happiness, but never lasting joy. One can NEVER find happiness outside of oneself. Their straightforward simple logic is "How can you ever FIND anything where it is not? Look for it where it is - namely WITHIN YOURSELF, and discover the Amazing Truth about who you truly are- A Spark of the Divine- That Divinity which is Itself All Happiness and Joy and Bliss! How can you ever hope to fill a cup which is already full? (The Great Saint Sri Ramana Maharishi's ONLY advice to his devotees was 'Find out who you are') It is certainly not an easy task, but that is no excuse for not trying to contemplate on and understand your true Identity or your TRUE SELF, as opposed to the false identity which you have been holding on to, all along- Your EGO SELF.

The majority of us are aware of only one aspect of ourselves- the physical aspect, consisting of our outward appearance, name, status, profession and so on. This is our little self /false self / ego self / physical self or worldly self. (call it by any name). But, underlying and beyond this apparent self lies our TRUE SELF- which is our Real Self, our Spiritual Self. It is a pity that many of us become apprehensive and even skeptical on hearing the word 'Spiritual' and falsely assume that it is synonymous with Rishis,Saints, Sanyasis and Gurus, and only meant for the senior-nay- super senior citizens! Spirituality is nothing but the knowledge that there is something greater than our mere mortal and temporary physical bodies that go on changing; and then trying to know what the permanent factor is. Certainly everybody will agree that there is some other powerful force in and around all of us. It is that force within us which enables us to live and act in this world...enables the eyes to see, the skin to feel, the mind to think, and so on. It is that force around us that makes the plants grow and bloom, the stars shine, the birds fly- in short that which operates the entire cosmos. This subtle force or energy or Intelligence cannot be seen by our limited gross physical vision, but we know it is there, flowing in and through everything in the Universe. We do know that every cell in our body, dies, and new cells are born every minute; we do know that we have changed from a baby to a child, an adult, then to an old man. These happen throughout, but they are all only your outward physical changes (mind included). Inwardly, there is something very subtle within you that remains as is, as a sort of substratum through all the changes and that Unchanging something is the Real You, Your Awareness, Your Consciousness, Your Higher Self or Your Spiritual Self. This is your Divine aspect- that Truth or Reality which is present in each and every unit of Creation. One need not go searching for It. We have to only remove the layers of ignorance that we have covered It with. Once the Ignorance is removed the True Self shines forth in all Its splendour. The renowned spiritualist, Dr. Wayne W Dyer calls this as the Sacred Self. He states that this Divine Energy has two aspects- the outer aspect that causes the heart to beat, the senses to function and so on, and the inner aspect that is generally dormant, but which can be awakened when you discover Your Sacred

Self. And when awakened, a whole new life full of Bliss awaits you. You can then transcend your ego dominated life, and live in a more enlightened way. This is really what Spirituality is all about. It is just being aware of and surrendering to a Higher Power that runs the Entire Show of Creation, and trying to get Connected to it. This is the Inner journey of Enlightenment, which will, by default, expand the God-like qualities like Love, Forgiveness, Kindness, Serenity etc in you. More than this, it will also help us to solve most of our problems. Problems may still continue to exist- but our approach to them will be far better, tackling them with a calmness and confidence and above all an inner strength, and not being bogged down and stressed out. Most of our sorrows and problems arise because we have wrongly identified ourselves with this perishable physical body and an unguided mind. Once this mistaken identity is removed, the Higher Awareness/Divinity in us becomes clearer and the journey Upwards, easier.

How do you start the process of awakening your erstwhile dormant True Inner/Higher Self? Below, I have given a few tips which have worked for me. There are many more and each one should try out what works best for him.

1. Set aside at least 10-15 minutes each day for yourself. Slowly increase it to half an hour to 40 minutes twice a day, if possible. Choose a favourite quiet spot , and choose a time of the day when you can get total silence. Early mornings

are the best, but not an absolute must. Since I have a separate pooja room, I prefer to sit there with an agarbathi (incense stick) lit. This action acts as an announcer to my mind, that my Private time has started, and it better pack up all its other activities and participate totally with me! Sit in a totally comfortable posture- the only condition is that the back/spine has to be erect. Eyes lightly closed, hands comfortable on your lap. Relax all the muscles. Silently observe yourself. This can be construed as the beginning of a simple meditation. (The real Meditation however has to be initiated by a trained Guru, with a proper Mantra). Just observe yourself and your thoughts. Dont bother to analyse, judge or even encourage them. Just OBSERVE them as a Witness or a Sakshi. Remember, your thoughts are NOT you. Begin practising stepping outside of yourself as a mere witness. The more you are able to develop the witness attitude, the more you will see that your attachment to your ego self, slowly takes a backseat, your sense of detachment increases and observation of yourself grows. The witness posture introduces you fully to your Real Self. It becomes easier now to start believing that You are not your problems, your frustrations or even just your physical self, but merely an observer of these things....just a sakshi. You are actually something more than your thoughts, feelings and sensations. This is because Your Higher Self slowly begins to influence your little ego self.

2. Make Nature your Best friend. Have a loving Communion with it whenever you can. Going for walks in parks and paying attention to and enjoying the beauty of the plants, flowers, grass, chirping of the birds, even children laughing and shouting with carefree glee, gazing with wonder and awe at the vastness of the ocean, the continuous rise and fall of the waves, looking lovingly at the blue sky with its twinkling stars, appreciating the myriad colours of pretty flowers, and a million other things like this. All this brings you nearer to your Higher level of Consciousness.

3. Firmly believe in and acknowledge from time to time the Divinity within you. The more you start believing in and asserting your Divinity, the easier it becomes to realise that you are not just this limited physical self, but far more than that.

4. Declutter your mind of all the unnecessary baggage that you are carrying. Learn to let go... The mind is a storage of past experiences, memories, and all the emotions and impressions that accompany them. We are thus often agonised with bad experiences of the past, the so called injustice done to us etc. These are the things we

have to learn to let go. Learn your lessons from the past, and leave it after that. Do not carry the burden of it with you indefinitely. And what you think of as 'injustice' could mean you just got what you deserved, not what you desired... which is the Divine Law. Similarly, don't worry excessively about the future. A certain amount of planning is necessary, but 'worrying' or being anxious about it is useless, and even harmful. These thoughts only clutter our minds and prevent us from living in the present moment where opportunity and creativity lie. They just dissipate your energy and cause your stress to increase. Try to be in the Present.

5. Instead of going on resisting, try accepting people and situations to the extent you can.(This does not mean you have to be a doormat; you have to lay restrictions and be firm about your convictions). But when certain unchangeable situations present themselves, instead of feeling crushed by it or adamantly trying to resist it, it is better to accept them as the Divine interference, and see how best to tackle it. Most of our sufferings are caused by a resistance to "What is". Acceptance on the other hand is letting things flow. It means to just see things as they are. A rose is a rose is a rose.

6. Try to avoid the company of people who cause a negative influence on you. Conversely , try to

read, listen to or if possible be in the company of great spiritual masters. This will increase your positivity, and bring you closer to your Divine Self.

7. Regularly practice yoga, or at least Pranayama. Prana is the Universal energy or life force. Without this, we would not be conscious. 'Pranayama is the bridge that one must pass over to get from physical consciousness to our Divine awareness within' - Sri Daya Mata, Disciple and Successor of Paramahansa Yogananda.

These are some tips that will lift you UPWARDS in life - reduce your Ego Self and increase the Divine Self in you. You know your Higher Self is dominating in you whenever:

1. You have a strong feeling of empathy towards someone helpless and you go out of your way to help him.
2. You feel a sense of gratitude towards your helpers- maids, cooks, drivers, gardeners etc, and appreciate them with words, gestures, gifts etc, instead of feeling bossy and proud that you are the boss and they are the servants.
3. You feel peaceful, happy, contented, confident, forgiving and letting go, looking for ways to help people instead of trying to take revenge.

Conversely, you can be sure your ego dominating self has taken hold of you, when you feel the opposite of the above mentioned things- fear, anger, jealousy, selfishness, anxiety, sadness, hopelessness, greed, avarice and so on.

Life can be enriched with lasting happiness and peace. All we need to do is to remove the ignorant and false identification of ourselves, as a mere limited mortal, and try to connect to that higher aspect of ourselves. Constantly look out for the above mentioned signs in ourselves, and try to increase and experience the Divine Awareness within ourselves. The Ego Self will not easily accept defeat, and will pop out its head now and then, but with continued perseverance we can alter the ratio. Over continued practice, the path becomes easier and the footsteps quicker.

"The mind has its source in pure consciousness, and once you are settled in pure consciousness, you automatically identify with your true self. And the glimpses of the true self will become deeper, more frequent and more lasting 'Deepak Chopra.. Having understood the need for identifying ourselves with the Higher Reality, let us now try to investigate whether it is Religion or/and Spirituality that will take us there.

Hari Om Tat Sat

9
Religion and Spirituality

Both religion and spirituality are two sides of the same coin- the coin that brings us closer to our own Divine Self. Both agree that there is a Higher Power, running the whole show in this universe, and unless we consciously connect with It, we will remain unfulfilled. However, the approach is different.

Religion, as we all know, is a set of organised practices, beliefs and rules to worship a God or group of Gods. - thus we have Christianity, Buddhism, Hinduism, Islam etc. Each has its own leaders upholding the formal aspects and rituals. The followers simply and obediently believe and follow the rules, either through sheer habit, commitment, fear of either being punished by God, or being frowned at. by society. Religion is objective, involves more of outward practices- like going to a temple,church or mosque, fasting on certain days or months, performing the prescribed religious actions like daily prayers, worshiping the various deities, japas or mantras-. Religion is certainly easier and more tangible and concrete-you have a fixed image, gods and godesses, and rules are already made, so, you just have to believe and follow them, and in return you get a lot of comfort and fulfillment.

Spirituality however follows a different approach- it is an independent inward journey. The urge for spirituality is inherent in people. There comes a stage in one's life when we find that all the material things in the world cannot give us permanent happiness and that life itself seems to be meaningless,and purposeless. And then starts the process of Search -The search for a deeper meaning, direction and Truth. Thus spirituality is born. Spirituality is not as "frightening" as many skeptical people think it to be. It is simply a realisation and acknowledgement of something more than what meets the eye and that you are also a part of that.

The process here is not about following someone else's beliefs, but trying to find your own independent conclusion, by going inward and searching for that Great Truth about who you really are. It is more of an understanding and inward progress, rather than belief or outward worship. It is basically a self introspection, empowering people to find their own beliefs and discover their connection with their own soul/atma and be attuned with one's inner self. With Spirituality, there is no limit, as one can broaden one's horizons and discover the potential of the Spirit within and relate it to the Spirit that permeates throughout- in Nature, in other human beings, animals and even in the mineral world. Spirituality teaches one to listen to the inner voice and use it as a guide to good living. Thus, Spirituality is Subjective, focussing on the internal aspect, and abstract, with no definite structure or tradition and purely based on understanding. It is a quest for inner meaning, direction and Truth, which is inherent in everyone. One must remember that Religion and Spirituality are not mutually exclusive. There can be spirituality without religion, religion without spirituality or both can exist together. It's your choice.

The marked difference between them, according to "Live and Dare" is:

- Religion asks you to believe. Spirituality asks you to look.
- Religion has dogmas. Spirituality has wisdom teachings.

- Religion wants obedience. Spirituality wants experimentation.
- Religion speaks of sin and hell. Spirituality speaks of karma.
- Religion wants to comfort you. Spirituality wants to liberate you.
- Religion is external. Spirituality is internal.
- Religion is the form. Spirituality is the essence.
- Religion wants to convert you. Spirituality wants to inspire you.
- Religion is an institution. Spirituality is a journey.

To decide which of two is more preferable, an analogy is helpful.

Just imagine you are standing on the ground and you have to enter a slightly elevated house. It has 2 steep steps. You have to climb both the steps. Which step would you say is more important?The first or the second? I'm sure you got the answer. Yes, both are needed. Initially, it is the first step. Exactly like Religion- since it's simple and tangible-something that can be easily understood and followed. Religion is like the first step. Thus, religion and religious practices certainly have a place in one's life. It is a starting point, disciplines us and helps to comfort us in times of hardships. Unfortunately, many so-called religious people think that the buck stops here - they think of this first step as the final step too. Worse, they even manage to distort religion and become fanatics, creating hate and enmity among one another. They forget that the goal of all religions is only to make one spiritual. Jesus, Prophet Mohammed, Guru Nanak, Saint Kabir, Swami Vivekananda, Rabindranath Tagore, Swami Mukundananda and many more- all of them advocated the Spiritual hallmark of love for all mankind-. Religion is only a means to an end and certainly not an end in itself! Religion has to progress toward Spirituality. In fact, the goal of all religions is ultimately to make one Spiritual. Your feet have to be lifted and moved on to the next step to reach the house. To extend the analogy further, many of us are still in the grey area- one foot on the first step and the second foot on the second step! We try to become spiritual and at the same time we are not ready to give up religious practices altogether- That's fine too...as long as we spiritualise religion , and not misuse it or become fanatics. Spirituality and Religion are not enemies-they do have common goals. But it is ONLY Spirituality that can lift you to the highest realm of Self Discovery, and reveal Your Divine Nature. It is only when we imbibe and exemplify spiritual qualities of inner purity, show love and kindness to all, serve humanity and above all introspect and Realise the True Divinity within us, and in every other person- it is only then that we have climbed onto the next step, and can enter the house.

The next crucial question arises -What does one have to do to become Spiritual? As Lord Krishna says in the Bhagavad Gita, Spiritual practices can be done in different ways, depending on the personal traits of individuals. For the emotional type of people- it can be through **Pure Devotion**-(like Meera) wherein your ego is dissolved and you merge yourself with the Divine, and allow the pure love to radiate throughout. (In this path of devotion and worship, only the purity of the mind is important- not the external paraphernalia that is seen in today's worship. Lord Krishna Himself has said – 'Patram, pushpam, phalam, thoyam- verse 26 Chapter 9, of the Bhagavad Gita. A leaf, a flower, a fruit or even just water- whatever my devotee offers with love and devotion,I will be greatly pleased'. Of course there is nothing wrong with external practices if they are going to help you to focus better and make your mind more pure. But if they are done just for show, it is of no use.

For those people who have more of Rajasic quality- i.e **action oriented**- their spiritual practice could be through pure, unselfish actions without any expectations, (Work is Worship- like Mother Teresa).

For the those who have more of Satwic Gunas- the intellectuals- there is **the path of Knowledge**- Intellectual self- reflection and realising our true divine nature with the help of our great Seers and Masters and their teachings, studying and reflecting on the great scriptures, etc (like Sri Ramana Maharishi). Meditation, and Yoga including Pranayama are also great tools to gain Spiritual Knowledge. Of course, a combination of all the paths is the most ideal, since an average man cannot compartmentalize himself into one particular group. Sometimes the call of the heart or mind (emotions) is stronger than that of the intellect (practical). Depending on the nature of his dominant trait of the moment, he can undertake his Spiritual practice.

Gone are the days of blind faith and belief. Today is the age of rationalism and scientific proofs. Hence, a more appropriate path would be Spiritualism-which involves solving the inherent truth to the enigma and meaning of life in a scientific way. To this end, our concepts of meditation, karma, reincarnation and enlightenment play a very great role.

What is the hallmark of a religious or spiritual person?

A truly religious or spiritual man is calm, peaceful and neither joy nor sorrow can adversely affect him. He is aware that his cup of joy is overflowing. He is at peace at all times with himself, knowing for certain the truth in the great Vedic Mantra -

oṃ pūrṇamadaḥ pūrṇamidam pūrṇāt pūrṇamudacyate .

pūrṇasya pūrṇamādāya pūrṇamevāvaśiṣyate .

oṃ śāntiḥ śāntiḥ śāntiḥ ..

Meaning, that he, as an individual soul is as Whole and as Perfect as the Divine Supreme spirit. He has learnt the art of attaching himself more and more to his Sacred Nature within.

In order to facilitate this transition from the mere physical to the ultimate Divinity within us, we have to educate our mind and intellect.

And to explore these inner equipments, let's understand them and then proceed to train them.

Hari Om Tat Sat

10

Mind and Intellect

According to the great Spiritual Leader, Swami Chinmayanandaji, every human being is made up of 3 basic aspects- the gross body,that we all can see and feel, and the subtle mind and intellect, which we cannot see or feel, but we know that it is there. Of course we all know enough about the gross body and how to take care of its various aspects. But, when we come to the more subtle aspects of our mind and intellect, very few of us know what exactly it is and much less, how to take care of it. Hence, the need to introspect and analyse. The most important thing to remember is that WE ARE

NEITHER THE MIND NOR THE INTELLECT, though they play an all important part in our lives.

Our whole life is but a storehouse of experiences. These experiences arise from our sensory impulses caused by our various sense organs. It is the **Mind,** that receives the stimuli and directs them to the intellect, under normal and calm circumstances. It then receives the carefully analysed response from the intellect and accordingly sends the replies or actions to be executed to the respective sense organs. Mind, is the seat of various thoughts, emotions, impulses and feelings. All our feelings and emotions of sadness, happiness, anger, jealousy, fear, likes and dislikes etc arise only in the mind. It is our best friend when it makes us happy, fulfilled, peaceful or serene- for eg. When we see the beauty of creation,we become filled with a marvel of happiness, or, when we achieve or do something great or noble, you experience a great fulfilment;- joys like these happen in our mind alone, and we should be certainly appreciative of this. Thus, the mind can be our best ally. Conversely,it can become our worst foe, destroying our peace and happiness, when it is filled with negative thoughts of anger, fear, hatred, greed, jealousy etc.. It is this negative aspect of the mind that we have to guard against. You see, the mind is like a child, and generally weak. It can fall a prey to the 5 senses which run helter skelter like the wild horses shown in the famous picture of the Lord Krishna driving the chariot, in the Bhagavad Gita, and has to be controlled.

The mind is defined as just a flow of thoughts, just as a river is a flow of water. The thoughts flowing in our mind, are just the manifestation of our desires. If there is too much water in the river, it overflows, causing a lot of damage. Similarly, too many thoughts crowding the mind, agitates and disturbs the mind. They have to be controlled by the intellect.

Intellect, on the other hand, is also constituted of thoughts. But, unlike the mind, which is always in a state of confusion, not knowing what to do, or just doing something just because you feel like doing it, the intellect analyses and comes to a rational decision and stabilises the thoughts to form a willed judgement. It is an equipment for the Higher Self to manifest. It is the seat of Logical Thinking, Reasoning, Judgement and, Discrimination. It is Strong (unlike the mind), and like the strict father, disciplining the errant child, the mind. (Intellect is different from intelligence. Intelligence is the ability to acquire knowledge and skills. However today, the usage of both these words- intellect and intelligence - are sometimes synonymous.).

There is thus, a world of difference between the two. There is also a strong inverse relationship between the two. **The higher the mind, i.e emotions, soar, the lower the intellect falls.** There is an Eternal War always going on between the mind and the intellect.And we must always ensure that the intellect is the winner!

As mentioned earlier our entire life is nothing but a series of experiences- and every experience is caused by the outer world of stimuli- which reaches us through our various sense organs- eyes, ears, nose,tongue and skin. These stimuli are then transmitted to the brain (in the physiological sense) or to the mind- the inner point of focus. (in the spiritual sense). Under favourable circumstances, i.e when the mind is calm, it does not respond or react at once, but allows the stimuli to be rationally systematised by the intellect- It is this discriminating factor, the reasoning capacity of the intellect- that makes us think and guides us as to what is right and what is wrong. The more strong and intelligent your intellect is, the better the judgement. The intellect then gives a suitable response to be given out, through the mind to the sense organs.

Unfortunately, this is not always the case with everyone, and even for the same person, not at all times. Quite often the mind takes the Power in its own hands and even before the intellect can intervene, it reacts hastily. And then you know the result. Total Chaos! Thus the wandering, wavering, sensuous mind which is responsible for all our sorrows and sufferings, should be guided and disciplined by the Intellect and made to attune with the Higher Nobler Divine Self in us.

Of course, each individual does have his own inherent range of weak or strong mind or intellect, with which he came into this world. But this is no excuse for complacency.

The main reason we have been given this human birth is to raise ourselves higher, spiritually from whichever level we are. It is our duty to analyse ourselves, find out our strengths and increase them, find out our weaknesses and decrease or even overcome them. We have to strengthen both our mind and intellect. Only then can we grow Spiritually, and lead a life of Peace and Happiness.

Our intellect, being the equipment for our Higher self to Manifest, can be best strengthened by Meditation. Apart from this, yoga- especially Pranayama, positive thinking, reading Spiritual books and contemplating on the Higher truths and above all, becoming more aware of the Divinity within us- all these are very helpful to strengthen our intellect and make it freely available to us at all times.

The mind, which is more difficult to train, can be strengthened by the following strategies:

1. Keeping a constant watch over the thoughts and nipping the unhealthy ones in the bud..i.e. as soon as they arise in the mind.
2. Plunging into activities that are for the general good, i.e without selfish motives, or any expectations whatever..
3. Keeping your mind busy in a constructive way.. (Even learning a new skill) An idle mind is a devil's workshop. Hobbies like gardening,

painting, listening to music, reading etc. are also a great way of strengthening your mind.

4. Distracting your mind from the lures of the senses - by deep breathing exercises, walks in the open, along with a child-like wonder and appreciation of the beauty of Nature.

5. Taking time to logically analyse your negative thoughts, like anger, hatred, jealousy etc. whenever they arise, instead of immediately reacting to them. Try to include a lot of understanding and empathy, if these negative feelings are against an individual.

6. Maintain a written record of your unhealthy thoughts and how you can tackle them.

7. Convince your mind to develop some positive thoughts and acts- like Contentment, Forgiveness, Empathy, Charity, Acceptance etc.

8. Self affirmation and conviction - This is another technique- Say, for example, you want to get rid of anger - first affirm to yourself- 'whatever happens, I am not going to get angry today'. If by chance you are provoked by someone- your earlier resolution will help you. Just quietly walk out of the place if it is possible. Else analyse and convince yourself- 'what's the use? The other person is not even going to be affected.

Ultimately, I will be the sufferer- my mood and my health alone are going to suffer'.

There may be more techniques - and each one should experiment and see what works best for him. Whatever it is, a lot of patience is needed to train the mind. Perseverance is the key. Training the mind is certainly a herculean task, but not an impossible one. Persistence is the password. Always remember, if you can master your thoughts, your mind will be an excellent servant- else you will always be a poor slave of your mind.

'The mind is a powerful force. It can enslave us or empower us. It can plunge us into the depths of misery or take us to the heights of ecstasy. Learn to use the power wisely- David Cuschieri'.

"Our intellect acts like a strong policeman, guiding and controlling the weak mind", says Swami Chimayanandaji.

Our aim should therefore be to chasten the mind and educate the intellect. To what extent can we make our mind and intellect stronger? Do we have the entire power to totally change them or is there something else that controls it? To analyse,let's take the next dose of multivitamins..

Hari Om Tat Sat.

11
VASANAS

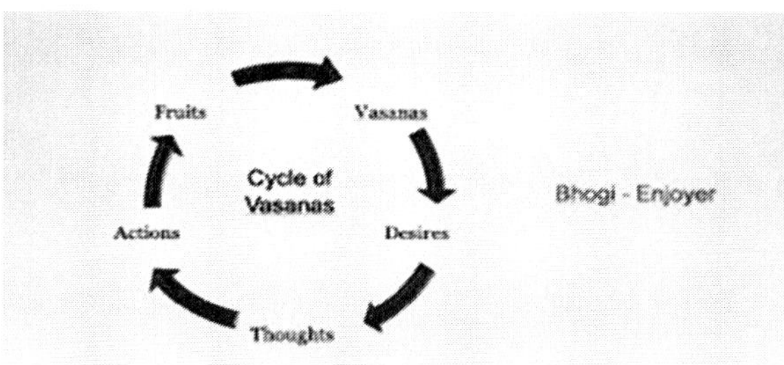

Closely related to the training of the mind and intellect, is another important aspect- Vasanas. Vasanas are just the past impressions of desires on the mind that influence the present behaviour. They are the latent or innate imprints which have been collected through various births, and faithfully carried on to the future births too, along with the mind and intellect. It is these three (vasanas, mind and intellect) that form the personality of man. They are dormant, unmanifested subtle energies, impressions, thoughts or inclinations, that have been gathered by our own desires in the past.

Vasanas are a reinforced or a group of **impressions**, (samskaras), that sink into the mind, caused by our various pleasurable or painful experiences. To elucidate - our whole life is only a series of experiences- pleasurable, painful or neutral. Pleasurable and painful experiences make an impression (samskara) on the subconscious mind, which is stored as memory. Many such experiences are latent. But, when they resurface (maybe even years later), they produce a desire to either repeat or shun the experience. When the pleasurable experience is repeated frequently, the impression gets reinforced (this is called Vasanas), it creates a strong 'like'. When an undesired experience is shunned frequently, it creates a strong 'dislike'. This leads to a habitual pattern of attraction and repulsion- likes and dislikes. The habit may be for both positive and negative samskaras. The negative impressions (samskaras or vasanas), are the ones we have to guard against, since they become deep seated cravings and results in a clinging attachment. It is a well known fact that the stronger the attachment, the greater the suffering. A person's mental disposition- positive or negative, thus consists of the accumulation of the mental impressions. It is this mental disposition that arises out of our vasanas, that primarily determines the type of reactions and responses to our everyday experiences. That is the reason why, given the same stimulus, different people react and respond in a different manner. For example, on seeing a rose plant with flowers, one person may admire the Marvel of

Nature and the beauty of the colours, another might think of worshipping his favourite deity with such beautiful flowers, a third one may just pass by, totally unaffected by it, and a fourth one might be analysing the sharp thorns in it! Same stimulus- different reactions. This is how Vasanas affect the personality of man. Vasanas are stored in the unconscious inner self, and form the basic inner drive that influences and affects future actions.

Vasanas are actually a hindrance to our spiritual growth, as it creates a strong, sometimes even helpless, desire in the mind and an attachment to those desires. Understanding Vasanas however, can be a great boon, as it makes one realise and empathise with the undesirable behaviour of others. When you realise that a person is a helpless victim of his bad habits, because of his past Vasanas, you can understand his helplessness, and even try your best to help him. Our whole attitude changes, when we realise that 'No man is born a sinner or saint. His earlier vasanas and present situations might have forced him to behave so'.

Vasanas are the seeds of desire. And desires, (good and bad) lead us to perform certain actions. Of course, having been born in this world, we Have to Act. (ref. Bhagavad Gita). But actions lead to more vasana accumulation. This is a vicious circle. Desires-> Thoughts-> Action -> Fruits-> Vasanas-> Desires. There is only ONE way to break the circle i.e perform actions and still not accumulate vasanas, and that is by performing pure, unselfish actions, for the general good and without expectation of any rewards- material, emotional or intellectual.

At the time of the death of the physical body, the dominant mental disposition is carried on to another body, along with our mind and intellect. Thus, we ourselves determine our next birth. In fact,they can be called the blueprints of our next birth. They determine one's physical, mental and emotional personality.and the field - the environment i.e, our own thought streams are responsible for the circumstances and also the major events that we will be experiencing in our next birth.

This is why we are repeatedly told to analyse ourselves and remove (or at least reduce) the negative thoughts, and increase the positive ones. Not only will we be happy in this life, but we can be assured of a good life in the next birth too.

Once this is understood, we can put an end to the oft repeated question whenever you face a problem - "Why Me??"

Our next step towards this goal will explore this avenue.

Hari Om Tat Sat

12

‘WHY ME’?

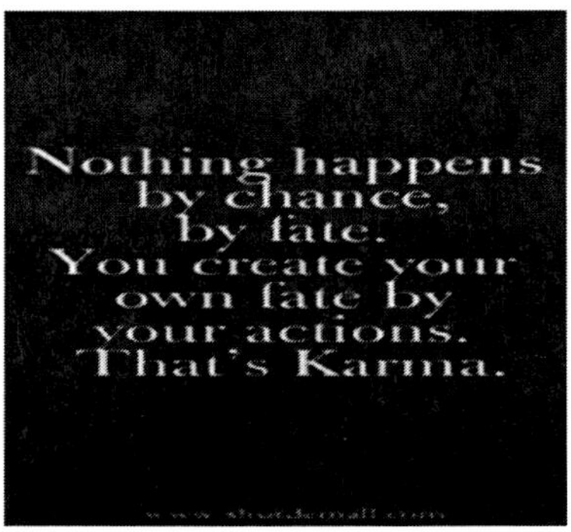

Indeed a frequently asked question, whether from an 8 year old or an 80 year old! And a very pertinent question it is.! “What did I do to deserve this? Why am I being singled out every time for ……..? Why does God make me suffer so much, in spite of me praying so hard? Why am I falling sick so often?” And a hundred similar questions and complaints. All sounds too familiar? Certainly we do find that the world is full of inequalities and injustice, and we wonder how God could be so unkind and unjust!

Well, there is only One pertinent explanation and the most satisfactory answer to this so-called 'unjust' treatment meted out to people, given by our great seers and saints and philosophers from our ancient Vedic Scriptures- One's own Karma. Though the word Karma itself has many different connotations, the one that we are concerned with now, is in the sense of the results of our actions performed. The law of Karma is the natural law of action and reaction. We are familiar with the saying what goes around, comes around. In physics, this is expressed by Newton's law of motion- for every action, there is an equal and opposite reaction. In Christianity we have the saying, "As we sow, so shall we reap".

(Karma, simply put, is 'Actions'. Now, Actions are the insignia of Life and having been born in this life as a human being, no one can escape doing actions (Bhagavad Gita). At the same time, the law of Karma stipulates that everyone has to experience the consequences of whatever actions he performs. Again, performance of actions are mostly based on one's latent vasanas or tendencies, which he has been accumulating from several births. And, actions lead to accumulation of more imprints- latent or expressed. In other words, one has to act and one has to also reap the consequences of his actions- both of the present and the past lives. What a tall order! However,this is not a threat, though one may feel so, since

today, karma is generally talked of in a negative way. It is not so).

Karma refers to good as well as bad actions- and actions, as such are performed by us only because of our inherent tendencies or vasanas. Another aspect of Karma is that it is only because of our Karmas (both good and bad) that the cycle of life continues and we are reborn on this earth, after death. Karmas are like a chain (maybe a golden chain for the good karmas and iron chain for the bad karmas) that bind one to the cycle of births and deaths, and prevent his Ultimate Merging with the Absolute. Only the actions of an Enlightened Soul will be free from karma and the resulting bondage.

Now, let us now go deeper and understand the" Why Me- I've done only good actions?" part- or why bad things happen to good people and vice versa.

An enlightened Soul, a Great Seer and Saint, His Holiness, The Great Adi Shankara says :

"Karma, in the sense of results of actions performed, is divided into three categories :

Sanchita Karma- it is the sum total of all the accumulated results of actions performed in the numerous past births.

Prarabdha Karma- It is those results of past actions which have given rise to the present body. It is a portion of Sanchita Karma taken for the present birth. (It has to be exhausted in this birth itself.)

Agami Karma (or Kriyamana/Vartaman Karma)- It is the result of the actions performed in the present birth that will come to fruition in the future. .

(When a person becomes an Enlightened soul, with the knowledge of Self- Awareness,, Sanchita Karma is completely destroyed along with Agami Karma, acquired up to the time of attainment of knowledge.After the dawn of the Self -knowledge, any action performed does not produce any result in the form of merit or demerit.- no more vasanas are created.

However, Prarabdha Karma is not destroyed even on the attainment of Self- knowledge, but has to be exhausted only by being actually experienced. *On the exhaustion of this karma, the body of the enlightened person falls off and the Jivanmukta (individuals liberation from this life) becomes a Videhamukta (Liberation after death- ending the cyle of rebirth).*

Adi Shankara further states that an enlightened person merely submits his body to the operation of the Prarabdha Karma".

(This explains why our great sages like Sri Ramana Maharishi or Sri Ramakrishna Paramahamsa cheerfully accepted their physical sufferings of cancer, and allowed their Prarabdha Karma to operate and get exhausted.)

There is a beautiful analogy to explain the 3 basic karmas. Imagine a quiver with a large amount of arrows in it. These arrows represent the Sanchita Karma (sum total of all the karmas- good and bad- in this birth plus from previous births). Out of this,now- ie in this birth, one arrow has left the bow and is on its way to the person concerned. This is the Prarabdha Karma, (results of the past actions that have to be exhaused in this life time itself). Nothing can be done except to experience it. It has to be worked out and get exhausted in this life. (This explains why so many 'good and innocent' people- even great saints like Sri Ramana Maharishi or Sri Ramakrishna Paramahamsa- suffer for no fault of theirs and conversely why so many 'bad' people get so much good fortune, even though they are doing only 'bad' things - they are all a result of the past karmas!) Next, A second arrow of the sanchita karma, has come out of the quiver and is about to be strung by the bow. But this arrow has not yet left the bow.This is Agami Karma (Agamani or Vartaman). Let me repeat- Out of all the accumulated Sanchit Karmas, a part has come out and is to be experienced in this birth - that is the Prarabdha Karma, answering the question "why me'. Another part has not yet come out, but will come out soon- this is the Agami Karma and it is this part that can be modified by us. Since this Agami karma refers to the future consequences of the present action, there is still a possibility of changing or softening the effects of this karma, by doing the prescribed actions , in this lifetime itself. That is why we are told to perform good actions, so that the ill effects of our earlier Sanchita Karmas which are about to take effect., through the vehicle of

Agami Karma can be softened or even nullified by these good actions.

Agami Karma can be further divided into -Aarabdh (sprouted) the arrow that is just leaving and its effects will be seen very soon (a good example is like that of a culprit, who has been caught red handed and is given immediate punishment) and Anaarabdh (seeded) -the arrow that has just left, but, whose effects may not be seen soon,(like that of the culprit who has escaped being caught, and hence is not punished), - nevertheless the effects of his wrong deed would get accumulated in the collection of arrows in the quiver- the Sanchita Karma, to be exhausted later on.

Thus, we see that there is no escape from any karma (good or bad) for anyone. (Except the Enlightened Souls, of course. Even for them, their prarabdha karma has to be worked out till the time of their Enlightenment or Self awareness.)The results of all our actions will come back to us some time or the other.

This is the only logical answer to Why Me? There is no God sitting High up in the Heavens and punishing the good and rewarding the bad! **We ourselves are responsible for all that happens to us.**

Our best option now is- Start with good and noble thoughts which will lead to good and noble desires, feelings and emotions and finally end in good and noble actions- actions done in a purely unselfish manner, for the greater good, and without an eye on the rewards. These noble actions will slowly wipe away your previous bad vasanas and karmas.

To what extent can we wipe away our previous vasanas and karmas? Are we not helpless victims of our previous karmas?

To explore this, let's take the next multivitamin and visit the land of realisation .

Hari Om Tat Sat

13

Destiny and Free Will

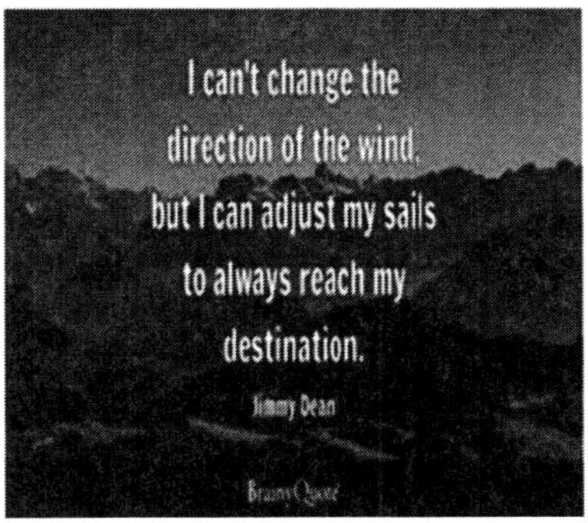

In the previous article ("Why Me?"), we learnt something about Karma. Let us now see how our Karma is related to our Destiny. Sister Shivani of the Brahmakumaris very beautifully said: "Whats happening to me as my destiny is a return journey of the energy that started from me- my earlier karma returning to me in the form of my destiny." This leads us on to a very crucial question. "Am I a helpless pawn in the hands of Fate or Destiny?

The answer is Certainly Not. No doubt your life is ruled to some extent by destiny- the destiny that you have created yourself. Thats why so many things happen in this world for obviously no fault of theirs. BUT, how you face that destiny, is your choice. You certainly can become a master of your destiny by exercising your self effort, through the choices you can make by your free will.! Sadguru Sri. Jaggi Vasudev asserts:" What comes in our way, is not in our hands- but what we do about it is certainly in our hands"! How empowering it is!

For a better understanding, let's delve into a few facts- our each and every thought (both good and bad) leads to desires and ends up in actions. They also create imprints or impressions (vasanas), which lie latent in our subconscious mind. They are carried through various births. In each birth one may add or reduce the number of vasanas, and carry the remaining vasanas to his next birth- and it is these vasanas that will determine his following birth. Thus, we make the blue print for our next birth through our own thoughts, desires and actions!

Now, "what goes around comes around". Accordingly, all the effects of the imprints in our mind from our past thoughts and actions, will come back to us as our own Destiny. As is the Karma, so is the Destiny. A portion of all the accumulated past actions (Sanchit Karma), will have to be faced in our present lives. There is no total escape from it. Its called Prarabdha Karma-

(this is the logic behind “why bad things happen to good people and vice versa or why a baby is born blind or deformed etc.). However, this karmic destiny can be reduced or softened to a great extent, by our noble efforts in the present- our self effort/will power. Not only that- the good actions we do in the present, will bear fruit, at some time in the future, This is called the agama karma. Thus, this is also in our own hands. How empowering!

To elaborate further, Destiny or Karma- is seemingly a fixed element- I say seemingly, since its already come to you and you have no choice but to accept it - at least for the present moment! For eg, you were born in a certain family, with a certain number of siblings, you have a particular physical feature that you might have inherited from your parents, grandparents etc, you were born in a certain socio economic society and so on.. These were your destiny. (Destiny is called as Prarabdha in Sanskrit) You did not choose them. They were pre destined.- Not by anyone else, but by your own past actions. As against this you have what is called Free Will…(called as Purushartha in Sanskrit) which enables you to choose- gives you a choice. With this choice of free will, one can alter one’s destiny to some extent. According to Sri Sri. Ravi Shankar, the destiny of your height cannot be changed, but the destiny of your weight can certainly be changed by your free will. Your inherited wealth is your destiny- but, whether you multiply it or lose it is your free will.

Another example is that of a cow in a field, tied with a rope 6 feet long. Being tied with a rope is its destiny. But in which direction it can go and for what distance upto 6 feet it can go, is its own free will and choice. If it puts in more self effort- like continuously mooing or struggling hard to free itself from the rope, it may even convince the farmer to extend the rope by another 6 feet! It has altered its destiny by its self effort!

Sometimes- when the forces of destiny are stronger, a lot more self effort is needed. Take the case of a gambler or an alcoholic- they have become so because of their destiny- their latent desires probably in one of their previous births, would have manifested in the present birth and made them so. Unfortunately, even after applying his free will and making a lot of efforts to change, he may helplessly go back to his weakness. The main reason for this is his earlier vasanas might be too strong, and this calls for more self effort.

Just remember: Your destiny is because of your past Karma, which can be mitigated through your present actions or karma and this same present actions or karma will also shape your future destiny. So, the need of the hour is to gravitate the mind (which is just a continuous flow of thoughts) towards good, noble, selfless thoughts (the basic foundation stone), which will then propel you to have those types of desires which in turn will give rise to pure actions. Then by default, you can become the master of your destiny.

Hari Om Tat Sat

14

ACCEPTANCE- A Key To Tranquility

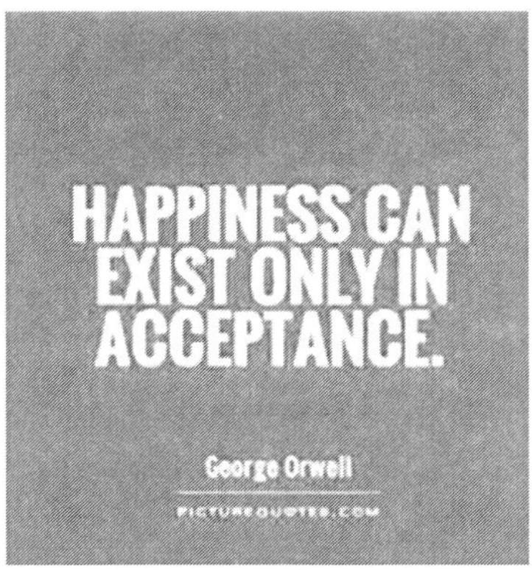

The majority of people have the wrong notion that just quietly **accepting** the so called disturbing elements in our life, is a negative quality pursued only by the cowards and the meek. It is not always so. Neither does it mean endorsement, approval, agreement, sanction or even tolerance. It is not a helpless resignation to something or someone. Acceptance is a great positive step towards personal growth and achievement. It is a gracious quality of intelligently understanding the scheme of things, and then surrendering oneself before the Law of Nature (The Divine Force). It is just a simple way of seeing things AS THEY ARE - A rose is a rose is a rose It holds the golden key to Tranquility and peace of mind. How? Just analyse carefully for a moment- How often has non-acceptance of a situation or a person's actions ever helped you? On the contrary it has only helped you to carry the wounds, sometimes for years- disturbing your mental peace, and constricting the free flow of happiness, which is your birthright!

Why do we always resist the 'behaviour' of other people or unfavourable situations in our lives? It's only because you are a victim of your own logic! Generally we tend to see things from our own perspective, our own jaundiced or judgmental eye, coloured with our personal likes and dislikes, ought to and ought not to! We have our own pre conceived notions of right and wrong, and when things or people or situations don't conform to them, we become upset and start resisting them. The result? Misery, frustration, anger and loss of peace. The remedy? Only a proper understanding and application of the magical formula- Absolute Acceptance-. ***"Serenity comes when you trade expectations for acceptance"*- Gautama Buddha.**

Basically, acceptance refers to two aspects- situations and people. If only we decide to "see" the various disturbing and painful situations - including our physical and emotional pains- the way they are, instead of resisting, resenting, fretting and fuming or looking for justifications, or asking 'Why me?", the seed of acceptance has been sown. Similarly, if we can calmly try to understand the people we are 'upset' with, in an empathetic manner, and with the awareness of "that's the way he/she is made", it will make a huge difference. Even with your own physical pain, if you first try to understand the 'why' of it and accept it, and then find a remedy, the results are much better than resenting and resisting and then trying to find a remedy for it. "Understanding is the first step to acceptance, and only with acceptance can there be recovery"- J.K.Rowling.

To begin with, try to understand that every person has come into this world with his own accumulation of tendencies and imprints (vasanas), and that's why his personality is what it is. To a great extent he may be even helpless about it. When we think on those lines, we become more empathetic, tolerant and sometimes even forgiving; and this attitude itself brings a calm and soothing effect on us too! Acceptance becomes easier and acceptance will, by default, lead to Love- the Mother of all Virtues! Always bear in mind that whenever you get angry or whenever you forgive, the effects, both good and bad, are more on yourself than the other person for whom it was intended! Thus, the secret of this strategy is that you start accepting, and when you accept, you LET GO!

The more you start accepting, the easier it will be for you to master the art of 'Letting Go'. And when this becomes an easy habit in you, you will emerge much stronger. However, the 'letting go' feeling should be for your personal self only. It should not be always expressed to the other party, because then, there is a risk of people taking advantage of your kindness. By all means, you can let the other person know that you are unhappy with his behaviour, but inwardly you should learn to forgive and let go- i.e not keep reminding yourself or carry the burden of revenge. It's not easy, but with patience and faith and above all trying to focus on the "present" and not dwelling too much in the past, you can master the skill of 'letting go'. Another strategy is to acknowledge your feelings of hurt or disappointment. Do not suppress them, but try to let out your feelings and emotions, by talking to a close friend, relative or even writing them down.

And when you are able to let go, you begin to relax. You may or may not still 'like' it , but it will certainly make you feel better and your unhappiness will be greatly reduced. Even for the most 'irrational things" (according to our views), there is no point in questioning or trying to reason out "why" (as it is impossible to fathom the plans of the Almighty). It will only result in more frustration, without doing any good -for ourselves or for others. Instead, things will be much better if you try to realise that **'situations and people have come into your life for a reason - to teach you a lesson, or**

as a result of your own past actions - and when the purpose is served, they will move away'.

Now, consider what happens when you, to begin with, Accept? It leads you to a state of mind that allows you to be peaceful. You become free of that internal stress, which is an inescapable result of any conflict or struggle. With that calm and stress-free mind, one can do wonders! This relaxed state of mind will give you an insight as to why that particular situation has come to you, or why you have to deal with such kind of 'conflicting' people, you don't like. One can then proceed to calmly analyse if it needs to be changed, or do we need to change ourselves and our views,and if so, how. **(A great Serenity prayer goes thus: God, grant me the serenity to accept the things I cannot change, the courage to change the things I can, and the wisdom to know the difference.)** Remember, that everything that comes to our life-situation or people- has a definite reason or purpose in our lives- it could be just a deserving fruit of our own actions of the past, or, to teach us a lesson or just for our own good. The best and most tranquil way is to gracefully, smilingly and willingly accept. Acceptance is not a cowardly act; it only means, arriving at a place of Peace; and being firmly rooted on this calm foundation, gravitate towards your goal.

That's not all. When you enter a deep state of calm acceptance, you open into a mysterious knowing that everything is fundamentally ok, and that this life is imminently trustworthy. A wonderful by-product of acceptance is that it will lead you to Equanimity- the golden rule for lasting happiness. Keeping your equanimity will see you through life's challenges. It's a pathway to greater peace, joy, calm, goodwill, integrity, balance, self-control, and higher potential. A composed and relaxed mind is a powerful mind. Equanimity is said to keep us on the right track in the face of eight worldly winds- praise and censure, gain and loss, success and failure, and joy and sorrow.

Learn to accept changes in your life--- change is the only permanent thing in life.

Learn to accept the situations and people in your life ----- they have all come with a specific purpose; hence try to analyse the reason behind this, and learn the lesson- you will rise in love.

Learn to accept your mistakes----- you become guilt free, and will set about setting things right.

Learn to accept your life -----Your ego will vanish and your true Self will start shining.

Learn not to have expectations -- you will have no disappointments and hence acceptance comes naturally.

Learn to go with the flow of life- go along with the current, not against it. The ride will become a pleasure!

Learn to let go of superficial desires - You will multiply your happines.

Learn to let go- you will live in love, harmony, peace and tranquility.

The next pill will take us to the land of 'Desires'.

Hari Om Tat Sat

15

Desires

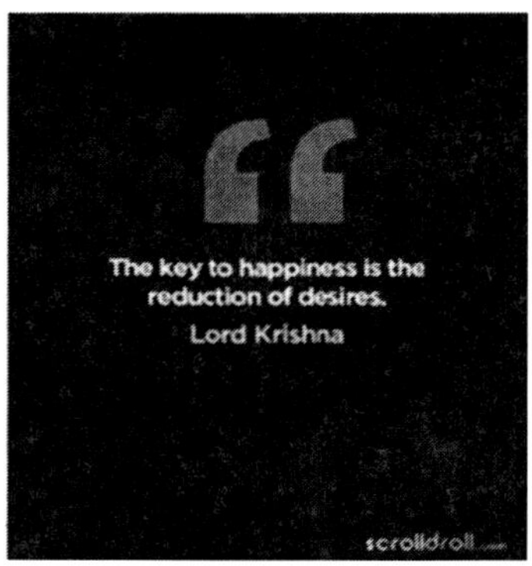

Our Vedas and other spiritual texts have emphatically declared that we i.e our True Self is a spark of the Divine, and, the moment we learn to associate our mortal selves with the Divinity in us, we can realise that we are already brimming to the full, and that we do not need anything more and hence desires have no place in our lives.

Unfortunately, this is not so in many cases, which is why Desires come into play. "We look before and after, and pine for what is not", said P. B. Shelley in his poem, To a Skylark. This 'pinning' leads on to desires and cravings, which ultimately robs us of all peace and joy. The root of any desire is the thought, and it is seated in the mind. Desires first arise as an innocent thought in the mind. If the thought is encouraged repeatedly, it blooms into a desire. It is best if we could analyse the thought before it turns into a desire. Not all desires are bad. Hence,the quality, quantity, need and the outcome of the desires have all to be borne in mind, before we encourage a thought to fructify into a desire.

The origin could be a present situation, an outward stimulus that has entered our mind through the sense organs, or the unfulfilled desires of the past lives, that have been latent so far and for some unknown reason, erupted again. Attachment to things or people is another propellor of desires.

Desires per se are neither bad nor good. It is like electricity. When used constructively, either for one's progress or in an unselfish way, for the good of others, it is laudable, since it goads you on to higher goals and propels you to perform progressive and noble actions. In fact, good, constructive desires are perhaps even needed for one's spiritual progress. There is another class of desires- small, innocent ones, like the desire for going to a movie, or having your favourite food. These are fine, as long as you do not overdo it, or start to crave for it. As long as you are the master of your desires, there is no problem. But once 'desires' start ruling you, you are bound to suffer.

The third type of desires, which are the most common, are the harmful ones, and that is what we should guard against. They are mostly materialistic, binding, harming oneself and others. They may give momentary pleasure but invariably end up in suffering. Desires are just like fire. The more you put into it, the more it will keep wanting. There is no end to it. This is because your satisfaction of these desires are directed at outward factors. And no amount of outward aspects can give you permanent joy. In fact, it only leads you to a vicious circle- the more you have, the more you want, and then you get more, but, the more you get, the more you want- the cycle is never ending. Another important angle to ruminate is this- Whether fulfilled or not, the end result of these material desires is always suffering. When fulfilled , it leads to greed, then avarice, then arrogance, then attachment, and then, the fear of losing. When unfulfilled too, it leads to disappointment, anger, jealousy, disillusionment, dejection and loss of hope. So, either way, it's a Loss-Loss situation!

How do we overcome the undesirable desires?

The foolproof way is the path of spirituality. When you meditate and attach yourself to the Higher Self within you, the Divinity within you, you understand that you yourself are complete and that you don't need anything from the outer world to give you happiness. Desiring anything from the material world will then seem too trivial and even purposeless.

Another method is to regularly train the mind to feel content. This might help to a certain degree, but the mind being a monkey, it's not an easy affair.

Yet another method is to distract oneself from the thought. It is said that a desire lasts for about 2 to 3 minutes, and if one is able to think of some other thing for those few minutes, the desire can be overcome. But this again is not a foolproof method, as the desire will resurface again, sooner or later.

Suppressing a desire also is useless, since it will lead to frustration and will start residing in the subconscious mind as an unfulfilled desire, ready to pop up at the first opportunity.

The best way to tackle desires is to **Transcend** the desire. This is not something new, as we have been doing it unconsciously since our childhood. The lower desires fall off automatically when you pursue a higher goal. The childhood toys dropped off when you played games on your computer. This desire too dropped in your teenage, when other desires popped up, and so on.

The secret is, you just need to hold on to a higher, more noble goal, for your lower desires to fall off automatically. And herein comes the role of the Intellect. Desires, when scanned by the mind give rise to lust, greed, avarice etc. But these same desires when scanned by the intellect can manifest as goal, ambition, mission etc. Hence, before a thought matures into a desire, ensure that it passes through the scanner of your intellect. The intellect alone can ensure that the desirous thought is an unselfish one, not merely for the selfish possession of worldly things and stands to the benefit of all.

The Bhagavad Gita, warns us to beware of desires- the greatest enemy (Chap.3) and tells us to control, reduce and finally eliminate them for total peace and happiness. "You are rich only if your assets are more than your desires" There is another beautiful saying - Happiness is : Amount of possessions divided by the number of desires. You can increase your happiness by increasing your possessions, (this involves a lot of outside factors) or, more efficiently, by reducing the number of desires (involves only yourself). Yet another thought provoking quote is Happiness = No. of desires fulfilled -divided by – no. of desires harboured. For more happiness, we may increase the numerator, but more importantly, decrease the denominator!

Think about it, till we take the next dosage.

Hari Om Tat Sat

16

Be Present in the Present

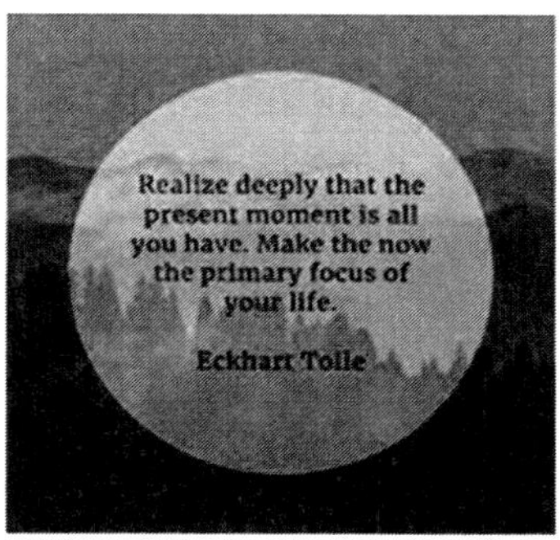

The primary goal of our existence in this world is to Realise who we TRULY are. It cannot be understood mentally, since the mind is just an instrument, and can comprehend only that which is objective. The Realisation, being totally subjective, can only be realised or experienced. The process of re-discovering our true essential nature, which is nothing but "A Spark of the Divine" (according to the great philosopher, Dr. Radhakrishnan) is the aim of all spiritual seekers.

However, there is one great obstacle to this and that is our own MIND. Somehow, from the beginning, we have created a mental image of ourselves based on this identification with the mind. This phantom self is actually called the EGO, which is only our false self. The mind is only an instrument, a faculty given to us, just as our limbs, organs etc. Of course it is more subtle than the gross physical body that we can see and touch, but nevertheless, still a tool, something that we all possess, and certainly NOT the real 'we'. What exactly is the mind? According to great thinkers, the mind is nothing but a steady stream of thoughts. And thoughts are the building blocks of our feelings, emotions, actions... in short all our experiences of life. Granted, all our discoveries, achievements, worldly conquests etc have their basis on thoughts. Our thoughts have the power to make our lives greatly advanced. At the same time it has the power to mar our lives also! Unfortunately, a majority of us are only victims of our thoughts. Very often, (about 80%) our thinking is either repetitive, useless and even harmful. It either broods about the past or fears about the future- both are unhealthy and can only destroy our peace of mind. When allowed to grow, these thoughts create reactions in the body in the form of emotions and actions. If thoughts are positive and constructive, fine. It is a blessing. But the negative and useless thoughts (which form the majority) can make our lives a real hell. The incessant mental noise is the greatest barrier to experience the STILLNESS of the mind, which alone can lead us to our inner realm of our true Blissful Nature. In fact, we have all become slaves to our mind. Thinking is no more under our control. We are helpless against the constant chatter of our minds. It is high time that we have to learn to use it as a tool - use it when needed and lay it down when not needed. But this is easier said than done!. Nevertheless, if only we try to learn the technique of how to control or regulate these thoughts, half the battle would be won!

A great technique, as explained very lucidly by a great spiritual teacher of our times- Eckhart Tolle, is to create small gaps in the mind stream, by using the **Power of Now.**. The technique is fairly simple, and can be regularly practised in our everyday life. You have to be INTENSELY CONSCIOUS of what you are doing at the moment. For eg. If you are washing your hands, just be aware of the sound of the falling water on your hands, the smell and lather of soap, the movement when rubbing your hands, feel the cool falling of the water again and so on. If you are writing on paper, watch carefully the way the letters are being formed by the pen on the paper etc. In this way we prevent the myriad other unnecessary thoughts which would fill up our mind. We draw consciousness away from the mind activity and help to create small gaps of no-mind, in which you are highly alert and aware, but you are not thinking. These small gaps are the initial steps to lead you to realise that your mind is not You. Try practising this as many times as possible. Personally I have found this very useful in another way also----- in case there is some work which is rather monotonous, (like cutting vegetables or arranging the cupboard, clearing up the dishes etc) but has to be done anyways, I employ this technique. Without a second thought, I just plunge into the act, becoming intensely aware of the shape of the vegetables, how it is being cut by the knife etc. The task is accomplished easily! And of course, by default, I have started to slowly dis- identify from the mind, which is what the author prescribes. The more frequently we practise this technique of being fully present in the NOW, the easier it is to overcome the 'pain' created by the mind. This is because, we are just concentrating on the PRESENT, the NOW, and not allowing our thoughts/ mind to go astray! All our suffering is only due to the PAST associations or FUTURE worries and fears, i.e we live exclusively through memory or anticipation! The EGO can only operate in the PAST and FUTURE, and can never operate in the PRESENT.

Thus, to remain free of pain and suffering it is imperative that we remain in the PRESENT for as much time as possible.

Strictly speaking,Time can be classified into past, present, and future. But this is only theoretical. In practical life there is only ONE time - and that is the PRESENT. Take a moment to think about this statement. Whenever any thought came into your head, or, whenever you had performed any action, it has always been in the present- the NOW! You might have thought about it, or done it at a certain time in the past, (with reference to this moment)...but isn't it a fact that when it actually happened, it was at that moment in the "present"? Similarly with the future. Your plans, worries, strategies, dreams, tensions, may all concern the future. In fact, most of them are only with regard to an unknown future. But when it actually is going to happen it will happen ONLY in a "present moment"! That's why great philosophers and thinkers have repeatedly advised us to take care of the present. Live each moment as it ought to be lived, rightfully and joyfully..and not brood about the past or worry excessively about the future. This does not mean that the Past and Future have no relevance at all! Of course, the lessons that the 'past' have taught us are certainly not to be ignored ; neither should we live in carefree abandon of the future. A certain amount of planning and providing for the future is surely necessary, but the problem comes when we go overboard, not realizing where to draw the line. We spend days and nights unnecessarily brooding about the past events, regretting about it, nurturing anger and hatred by repeatedly rewinding the unhappy scenes in our mental screen. Similarly, we become mental wrecks, worrying and stressing out about what is going to happen to our future, our studies, college admissions, careers, jobs, financial affairs, children, and even about grandchildren! What we gain by this ignorant living is only a long list of illnesses- diabetes, high B.P, ulcers, heart problems, etc etc.

What then is the solution to this malady that has afflicted almost all of us? How do we get out of this ingrained, almost subconscious rut that we have sunk into? The answer is simple. It is to become aware of a totally new dimension of time.

The great philosopher and spiritual writer Eckhart Tolle classifies 'Time ' into two categories- Clock time and Psychological time. Clock Time is the time that flows through every moment. There is No emotional charge in it. This is the 'time' we make use of in a practical way, to create the life that we want to lead. It is a wonderful tool to plan and execute our daily chores, and for the future goals as well. Clock time can also be a wonderful tool to help us peep into the past, realize our mistakes and learn from them. Thus, when we use time as a tool for our practical purposes, we use clock time.

On the other hand, Psychological time is the time we experience in our mind! When we dwell on a situation mentally, we drop off the present moment. We get stuck to the situation and lose the present moment which is so precious. This is the psychological time, and we have to be aware of it. Otherwise, we will only be either living in the past- with feelings of guilt, remorse, sadness, hatred, bitterness of the past events or living in fear, stress, anxiety, tension and worry of an imaginary projected future. Both are extremely harmful and rob us of the joy of living in the present. We get trapped in the mind, thus creating more problems with no solutions! Constantly projecting ourselves into and living in the past or future, can never produce any positive result or fulfill one's dreams and goals.

The answer is loud and clear. Be aware of Psychological time. Frequently stop to analyse the mind and reduce the amount of psychological time it gets trapped into, to the bare minimum. Simultaneously, concentrate on the action taken at each present moment, being fully aware of it, and focusing in depth at each step taken. This is the key to a happy, carefree and successful living! The Present Time is the Best time!

At times, it may happen that even the PRESENT experiences are very disturbing and painful- unpleasant and unacceptable. In such cases, the author Eckhart Tolle advises us to remember a great slogan, "IT IS AS IT IS", and keenly 'watch' the mechanics of the mind. Instead of resisting, if we just allow the present moment to be, accept it, and then work with it,doing whatever you have to do, you are likely to overcome it, or at least feel less disturbed. When we become the watcher of our mind's mechanics, the inner strength comes into play. When we identify with the mind, we begin to suffer along with the mind, we become restless, frustrated and, with such a mind no solution can happen...only more chaos. Accepting the present moment does not imply meekly and negatively resigning to the unacceptable or painful situations. One has to do whatever has to be done, take some action...if you have a headache, take the needed medication; if somebody is acting rudely, politely tell him it is unacceptable to you, or just leave the place; if you are caught in a traffic jam, and there is no way out, just bear with it,listen to some music, or just look out at other cars and people, without getting anxious or tense about what is going to happen....if possible you can contact the concerned person and explain the situation etc. But in all the cases the first thing is to ACCEPT the Present, not resist it. Then your false ego takes a beating, and a higher force comes into play.

Thus it is in the timeless NOW that we have the key to most of the problems. Of course it takes some practice and willingness to continuously stay in the present moment, but at least we can try to reduce to a bare minimum, the amount of times when we drift back to the memories of the past or in the projection of the uncertain future. (psychological time). It is the Present Moment that is inseparable from the Eternal, Ever Present Being or Divinity, which is actually our TRUE NATURE. But this TRUE NATURE of ours is obscured by the untrained Mind which has erroneously got connected with our outer personality and has become "the EGO", and projects only a false self. Hence it is high time we learn to dis -identify ourselves from our false-mind,and attach ourselves to our real Nature by harnessing the POWER OF NOW.

(Inspired by the book 'The Power of Now' by Eckhart Tolle).

Trust no Future, howe'er pleasant!
Let the dead Past bury its dead!
Act, --act in the living Present!
Heart within, and God o'erhead!

- H. W. Longfellow

Hari Om Tat Sat

17

Work and its Reward

In the Bhagavad Gita, (our greatest handbook for intelligent living) the Lord explains in detail about work, and how to perform it and declares that our concern should be only to work, and not about its fruit. This statement has evoked a lot of skepticismlet analyse this further.

Chapter 3 of the Bhagavad Gita discusses elaborately about work and how it is to be performed. Having been born in this world, work/performance of actions is a Must. There is no escape from it. However, selfless work, done in a dedicated manner,with sincerity, for the good of others and without any expectations is the best way to work. It can then be considered Worship. Furthermore, no work is considered high or low-whether it is a mundane work of sweeping the roads, or a highly sophisticated work of running a million dollar company, both are equal. It is the dedication and spirit of service, without any expectation of reward that makes an action meritorious

There is a great insistence on unselfish work .In chapter 2, verses 47 and 48, The Lord declares that our duty is only to act, never to be concerned with the results. In chapter 3 verse 3, chapter 4, verses 19 and 22 the same idea is repeated. In chapter 12, verse 11, Lord Krishna declares that even if a devotee can take a simple path like renouncing the fruits of his actions., he will be liberated.

How is it that 'renouncing the fruits of action' is given so much importance? Why is it said that we have to do our prescribed duties in life without looking for rewards? As kids we must have heard the quote "Do your duty that is best, Leave unto the Lord the rest." Is it really that simple or even possible?

At a cursory glance, it does seem rather impractical and even impossible. "How can anyone just do work without knowing what he is going to get in return? Is it really possible to go on doing work without any reward or gain whatsoever?" These are some pertinent and natural doubts and questions that will normally arise in people. But, they will easily fade away, when we carefully think over the matter.

On a deep analysis and intense study of our great scriptures, the profundity of the Lord's statement can be realised. Performing your actions perfectly should be our only concern. What the Gita advocates is that we should just do work for the sake of work, and not only for the sake of reward! Do the prescribed duties with full devotion, dedication and sincerity, putting your entire heart and soul into it and NOT with anxiety, fear, greed or even expectations about what its outcome will be, or how much reward there will be. This is the message of the Gita.

How is this such a powerful statement? Let us analyse:

1. "Fruit of an action is the action of the present moment maturing itself in a future period of time" says Swami Chinmayanandaji. In other words, action is in the present time whereas its fruit is in the future time. Now,isn't it true that, when the concentration is not 100% during the performance of the action,ie the present time,(since it is diluted by thoughts of 'fruit' which is a future event,) any action is bound to be flawed?

2. The unnecessary and imaginative anxieties and worries of the future outcome (negative tendencies) will certainly dissipate and rob you

of your present dynamic energy, rendering your work 'mediocre'.

3. The rewards and outcomes that you expect from the outside world, are certainly beyond you. You have no control over them. Whether its an exam you are writing, an interview you are facing, or a job assignment you have undertaken, the merits of your actions depend upon so many other people,so many factors and so many different situations. The futile anxiety and expectation over something which is NOT in your hands, is not only absurd, it will also ruin your health.

4. There is also the danger of 'wrong expectations", which will only cause dis-satisfaction in the end.

The declaration of the Bhagawad Gita is thus, undoubtedly undisputable. 'Work for the sake of work', 'work is its own reward' are not just idealistic statements. Practical examples can be seen in great artists and artisans. When a great artist paints a beautiful picture or a musician deeply involved in his art, performs, blissfully unaware of anything, he does not worry about its reward. He is thrilled and extremely satisfied with himself. He does not need to look outside for gratification. Similarly, if only we could learn to stop looking outside for reward-whether physical (monetary) or mental (fame & recognition) and rest content with the great self satisfaction of a job well done, we will have achieved our goal! It is somewhat like participation in some event which you like. You may or may not get a prize- but the participation itself gives you a great joy. It's quite possible that it may be a little difficult for the common man, at first, but certainly, by consistent effort, one CAN train his mind to do his prescribed duties in a spirit of willingness, just because it has to be done. When done with full dedication and sincerity, wholeheartedly and to the best of your ability, work itself becomes its own reward, giving you that supreme sense of fulfilment and self satisfaction. This should be our goal. And it is this sense of fulfilment that can give you Satisfaction and Contentment in the real sense of the term.

Contentment certainly is a great source of peace and happiness. But is that the final frontier? Let's take one more pill and examine.

Hari Om Tat Sat.

18

Contentment and Complacency

"Living without grumbling and complaining about life is Contentment". Being satisfied with whatever you have, or whatever action you performed to the best of your ability, is Contentment. But, there has always been a gross misunderstanding about this word. Not realising the power of this great attitude of the mind, which is one of the greatest precursors to Peace and Happiness, the ignorant confuse this with Complacency! They erroneously but vehemently believe and argue that if one is contented with what he has, he will never have any goals or ambitions, or ever aspire for more, and will only become lazy, uninspired and totally complacent. They have the baseless fear that in this world of stiff competition and opportunities, he would be stuck-deep down in the lowest rung of the ladder of success and ultimately, become a loser.

This is far from the truth! Being Contented is NOT Complaceny! In fact, Contentment and Complacency are two opposite poles. Contentment is a great positive virtue,giving great strength of mind and peace, and attracting to itself other positive virtues like simplicity, gratitude and compassion. It is one of the core values of the various spiritual traditions, and is considered as a virtue and a practice that leads to happiness and liberation. It is the key to overcoming the fluctuations of the mind and attaining inner stability and joy. It is not a complacent state, but an active and dynamic one that involves awareness, acceptance, detachment, effort, discipline and faith. In Sikhism, it is called as 'sahaj' and is the state of being in harmony with God's will. According to the Buddha, contentment is the source of spiritual power that enables one to achieve one's goals and aspirations. It teaches us the first law of personal growth - the Law of Acceptance, (where you simply see a thing the way it is). On the other hand, Complacency is a negative emotion, leading to laziness, apathy, idleness and sloth. While the first is a Satwic quality, the second is a Tamasic quality. Through ignorance, we misunderstand the nature of Contentment,or its extent.

A truly contented man, to begin with, should be able to see a thing as it is, and accept it as such. A rose is a rose is a rose. This is in no way a state of passivity. Once you accept, you let go, and in such a relaxed state of mind alone is it possible to climb higher. Again, contentment should be only as far as the fruit of his actions are concerned, knowing fully well that it is beyond his control. There should however be a "Divine Discontent", as far as his efforts are concerned. Fully understanding that there is always scope for improvement, he should put forth all his positive energy on more and more noble actions . His attitude should be like that of an optimist- happy and thankful for what he has, and at the same time enthusiastic to continue doing even more noble actions. He should have ambitions and goals but at the same time not be bogged down, worried or unduly pressurised by its outcome. With the strong foundation of contentment, there is a great peace of mind, unruffled, and this calm mind can put out more productive work. Work done for the sake of work, becomes a pleasure. His concern and one pointed concentration should be only on the discharge of his duties to the best of his ability, sans the pressure or worry about the reward. And this alone will fetch the best result. He has truly understood the words of Lord Krishna in the Bhagavad Gita. "Do your work to the best of your ability, do not worry about the fruit of your actions." Skeptics may argue that this is all too idealistic and not practical, but given a serious try, it can be made practical. The mind can be trained ...." After all, what is the point in brooding about the past or worrying about the future ('what fruit will my actions bear')? Isn't it better to just act rightly in the present?" His mental energy will be totally concentrated on his actions, and he will be supported by his own positive thoughts and inner strength. The quality of the efforts and actions will certainly be excellent.

Of course there may be some situations when there is some gross injustice done, and being contented then would be impossible. In such cases, it is better to acknowledge the injustice, and perhaps take some help from the saying that one gets what one deserves,not what one desires. This may be a little compromising, but it is certainly a better alternative than fretting and fuming and making yourself miserable. Discontent has never helped anyone. This negative trait has only helped one to be restless, uncertain, anxious, frustrated and stressed out, along with other negative traits, as each negative trait acts as a magnet to another. There will be a deep sense of regret of the past and a sense of anxiety of the future, worrying about the results, which is certainly not in his hands. Even if he does achieve some amount of success, being a basically discontented type, he would still not be satisfied, and, any action done under these conditions can never be well done. He would only end up being more frustrated and disgusted and take recourse to becoming more complacent!

Thus it is the Contented person who will become more fruitfully active, and it is the Discontented person who will become complacent! No wonder Benjamin Franklin said "Contentment is the Philosopher's Stone that turns all it touches to Gold"!

Dear reader, with this peaceful and contented mind, let's **Pause** a while. **Ponder** over the contents, contemplate over them and Practise them to the extent possible. But do Not be complacent and stop with this. **Proceed** on this Divine Path dedicatedly. A strong foundation has been laid. The right dosage of medication for an empowered mind has been given. It is now up to you to Progress further and construct your beautiful personality over it.

Hari Om Tat Sat

Conclusion

We have now ascended eighteen steps towards our sacred pilgrimage, and learnt the secrets of strengthening our minds. Each secret is unique, invauable and truly inspiring. I am truly grateful to all our great thinkers and revered Masters and to the various google sites that have influenced me a great deal in the making of this book.

'Some books are to be tasted, others swallowed and some few to be chewed and digested', said Francis

Bacon. This is to be included in the last category- chewed and digested. It has to be read slowly, repeatedly (chewed) and assimilated or put into practical action and experimented (digested) time and again.

By no means is this a complete treatise to realise that you are not just 'a self' but "The Self. This is just an eye opener to goad you on to search for That Ultimate Truth- That Divine Principle that rules everywhere and to realise that you too- just as the entire creation- are a speck of that Divinity.

This eye opener is just the beginning- to ignite you on to the path of understanding yourself and propel you on your onward journey towards your Destination of Realisation. The daily dose of multivitamins for the mind have been given. Try to allot at least an hour everyday (maybe even 30 minutes on very busy days) for any spiritual practice- reading, listening, contemplating, meditating, japa chanting or writing. This itself will build a strong foundation later on in life when you do have plenty of time and can extend your spiritual activities to a longer duration.

The writing of this booklet has indeed given me great joy and fulfilment. My inner strength and spiritual progress have expanded and there is a general feeling of goodness within. This is a sure sign of spiritual progress.

Let this little step be the **beginning** of your Sacred Journey. Relentlessly pursue this path. Remember the words of the Lord: **No Spiritual Effort will ever go in vain.**

May the Blessings of the Divine Shower upon us.

Hari Om Tat Sat

Nirmala Raman

Chennai, Aug '24.

About the Author

A devout meditator and an ardent spiritual seeker, Nirmala Raman has been an English teacher for more than 3 decades. Throughout her teaching career, she confesses , she has tried to instill in her students, the high values and insights of many great thinkers and writers more than the nuances of the language."It's a prerogative of the language teachers," she says.

Her writings, initially, were just for the sake of self fulfillment. Later on, she wrote articles in " The Speaking Tree", created some YouTube videos on The Bhagavad Gita and other topics, and has also done a few podcasts. Her mission in life now, "is to spread the divine words of wisdom of our ancient spiritual Masters, as revealed to them, in their moments of elevated conscience." Written in a simple, lucid manner, this book presents the reader with ample food for thought .